Book Synopsis

"Discerning God's Voice: Is It You Speaking Jesus?" is an intimate study of scripture detailing how to discern God's voice and prophetic words from the voice of people, society, influencers, witches, devils, and ourselves. Being able to discern properly is key to knowing which words to follow so that the fruit and fullness of our destiny and calling can manifest in the earth. It is also vital in this day and time where the word "prophecy" and "God said" is used so freely, and words actually sound like God speaking, but may not be from him. We are to "try the spirit" of words and to discern fruit, yet there is often a drive to follow one's desires rather than take the time to discern the origin, character, nature, and substance of a word. This book is designed to teach you to discern where you are not being tossed to and fro and led astray by your own will, the ways of others and the world, and destroyed by the devil. Decreeing an immediate SHIFT in knowing the voice of Jesus Christ as the revelation of this book empowers you. SHIFT!

TaquettaBaker@Kingdomshifters.com
(Website) Kingdomshifters.com
Connect with Taquetta via Facebook or
YouTube

Taquetta's Bio

Taquetta Baker is the founder of Kingdom Shifters Ministries (KSM), Kingdom Shifters Empowerment Church, and Kingdom Wellness Counseling and Mentoring Center. She has authored twenty-six books and two prayer decree CD's. Taquetta has a doctorate in ministry from Rapha Deliverance University, a Master's Degree in Community Counseling with an emphasis on Marriage, Children and Family Counseling, a Bachelor's Degree in Psychology and Associates Degree in Business Administration. In addition, Taquetta has a Therapon Belief Therapist Certification from the Therapon Institute, which provides faith-based counseling training and equipping to people and ministries.

Taquetta is also gifted at empowering and assisting people with launching ministries, businesses and books and provides mentoring, counseling and vision casting through Kingdom Shifters Kingdom Wellness Program. Taquetta serves on the Board of Directors for New Day Community Ministries, Inc. of Muncie, IN. In October 2008, Taquetta graduated from the Eagles Dance Institute under Dr. Pamela Hardy and received her license in the area of liturgical dance. Before launching into her own ministry, Taquetta served at her previous church for 12 years. She was a prophet, pioneer, and leader of Shekinah Expressions Dance Ministry, teacher, member of the presbytery board, and overseer of the Altar Workers Ministry. Taquetta receives mentoring and ministry covering from Bishop Jackie Green, Founder of JGM-National PrayerLife Institute (Phoenix, AZ), and was ordained as an Apostle on June 7, 2014.

Taquetta flows through the wells of warfare and worship and mantles an apostolic mandate of judging and establishing God's kingdom in people, ministries, communities, and regions. Taquetta travels in foreign missions and throughout the United States. She has mentored and established dance, altar workers, deliverance, and prophetic ministries. Taquetta ministers in the areas of fine arts, all manners of prayer, fivefold ministry, deliverance, healing, miracles, atmospheric worship, and empowers and train people in their destiny and life's vision.

Connect with Taquetta and KSM at kingdomshifters.com or via Facebook.

Reenita's Bio

Reenita Keys has an Associates in Business Administration and is pursuing her Bachelors in Business Administration with a focus on Marketing at Ball State University. She became a licensed minister in June of 2018 through Kingdom Shifters Ministries and JGM Prayer-Life Institute and is currently training for ordination in the office of a prophet.

Reenita is an entrepreneur who carries a prophetic mantle. She operates in the gifts of prophecy, dance, intercession, spiritual warfare, teaching, deliverance, healing, scribing, and marketing. Reenita has a keen seer anointing and has consistent dreams and visions that encompasses strategies for bringing heaven to earth, delivering people and regions, while overcoming demonic forces and strongholds.

Reenita is an Elder and leader of the Kingdom Watchman Prayer Team of Kingdom Shifter's Ministries. Reenita has a heart to see God's will to be established through preaching, teaching, equipping, and training up the next generation. She is a visionary and forerunner of her generation, who is the Founder and CEO of "Chaziy'el Armory." Chaziy'el Armory is a Christ-centered apparel company that brings forth the vision of the Lord through intricately designed clothing. Reenita plans to use her education, training and prophetic mantle for the advancement of *the Kingdom of God, while bringing a fresh breath to every area of the marketplace both spiritually and naturally.*

Connect with Reenita and KSM at <u>kingdomshifters.com</u> or via Facebook.

FOREWORD

We live in the era of apostasy!

What we call the Prophetic-Apostolic revolution is a far cry from what Jesus posited when he walked on the earth. As much as we wail and cry with lifted hands to God without learning to hear His voice, then our heads would be filled with noise from our bellies.

Call it the Laodicean Church, call it the lukewarm church, call it the perverse Church!
Whatever name you choose, what we see today is a backslidden and fallen Church that has ignored the voice of God completely, yet only turn to Him when we need Him as saviour but not Lord over our lives.

Unfortunately, this is the epidemy that has infested the Body and sadly the Charismatic movement has not helped at all, what we hear from the pulpit is quite sad, validating choices from our carnal selves which opposes the voice of God.

How do we go on about life without hearing the voice of God? The voice of God is our lifesaver. As I read this work, I am reminded of a driver who cannot find his way around and as he drives pass each street, trying to find the address but to no avail. Then comes the Satellite navigation, as he punches the zip code, then he is able to find his way. The Satellite navigation helps him find his way! This is how the voice of God works. God's voice is our life's navigation, helping us find out what He has purposed for us.

In their book; "Discerning God's Voice," Taquetta and Reenita clearly explain scholastically what it means to hear the voice of God. Their in-depth revelatory knowledge about this topic is amazingly outstanding.

They understand both the Greek and Hebraic etymological renderings of words which pertains to this topic in order to build a solid theological submission and present a user-friendly readable work!

An absolutely mind-blowing piece with great insights. I love how they identified spiritual gifts, but also provide strategic ways to validate their position. In their own words *"Strategy" helps you to resist being worried, fearful, inferior, and insecure as you know God's got you. He has given you a plan to keep you solidified in his secret place. You can work your strategy to remain fortified as God works his word for and in you."*

They explained in detail of how we can discern with our senses - I was blown away by the revelatory insight of the six senses and the role they play in discerning God. Sometimes we are distracted by our voices instead of hearing God speak to us.
Finally, a very timely word about discerning the voice of witchcraft words and demonic infiltrators of GOD'S word. This is one teaching in the Christian community that is underemphasized but this is just LIGHT. They gave excellent ways to identify witchcraft words and I must say: This is a brilliant piece.

In their words *"Yoga, Christian Yoga – Yoga is rooted in Hinduism and Spiritualism. Yoga practitioners encourage you to empty your mind; to release to a place of a blank mind. God tells us to have his mind and to meditate on him day and night. Even if you contend you are meditating on God, your positions say you are bowing to a Hindu God. Every pose has symbolism that is tied to mysticism, idol gods and demonic spirits."*
I have spent years bringing to attention the rise of false prophetic voices empowered by hell to negate the prophetic words of the true prophets.

They have also highlighted this concern too, and I must say this is an excellent read and five star worthy!

Dr. Oscar Guobadia
Apostolic oversight, The Brook Place
United Kingdom, London
www.thebrookplace.com

FOREWORD

I am honored that I was asked to write a forward for this book. As one who has walked in the office of Prophet for the Lord since August 1998, I found this book to be refreshing and a reminder that a Prophet of the Lord must never forget the do's and don'ts of the call. We must always learn to discern and discern to learn!

> ❖ *I say to those who think they have a prophetic call on their life,* **read this book**!
> ❖ *I say to those who walk in the office of the Prophet,* **read this book**!
> ❖ *I say to those who want to understand the prophetic,* **read this book**!

Why? Because it is full of nuggets that will transform your life, gift, and office! Each chapter will help you define areas that are much needed as you journey in the call that is on your life. Each chapter makes you evaluate yourself as one who embodies and releases the voice of God!

In chapter one a foundational truth of one who speaks God's word is revealed in the first sentence. It states, "*Just because a word of revelation from God is spoken does not mean it is a prophecy!*" I love to exhort and encourage people, and I do that with all my heart but I am not necessarily prophesying! Yes, I am a Prophet of the Lord but I do not always prophesy! But, because people do not have a full understanding of the PROPHETIC, they want to call much of anything God speaks prophecy! This book exemplifies revelation to identifying **"WORDS OF THE LORD!"** and gave a great rendition of *1Corinthians* by teaching people to distinguish how God speaks.

The revelation provided in this book regarding discerning through spiritual senses is exceptional. As a prophet, I use spiritual senses when ministering to people, especially when flowing through the gift of knowledge and the word of wisdom. As believers and prophets, we must have ears to hear, eyes to see, a touch to feel. We must be able to perceive when God is speaking and moving through our senses by the power of the Holy Spirit. Taquetta and Reenita yields revelation of how to discern as God leads, where his voice can be identified and made clear through believers and prophets.

The chapter on *Demonic Infiltrators of God's Word,* you see what we as Prophets and prophetic people war against, and how we must not be ignorant of Satan's wicked devices! The attacks against the word of God are very present. We must know how to discern the enemy and silence his voice while continuing to establish the voice of God in the earth.

Discerning God's Voice will be a book I will add to my teachings and trainings as I continue to raise up prophets and prophetic people in the earth! Prophets, Prophets in the Making, Prophetic People and for sure Pastors must read and be able to demonstrate the knowledge in this book by properly speaking and governing the voice of God.

In His Grace,
Prophet Cathy Fontenot
Living Praise Christian Church
Palmdale, California
www.jgmenternational.org

ENDORSEMENT

If you have a prophetic bone in your body, you will bubble up at every turn in this book. Your soul will be dissected as Taquetta and Reenita covers all areas of the mind, will, and emotions. They leave no stone unturned, using the Word of God as the great divider to bring precision and clarity to the voice of God versus any other voice. Absolutely nothing divides between soul and spirit like the Word of God, and she showers you with the sacred text. The reader is constantly being washed with the water of the Word, thus exposing the intent of your heart - truth triumphs. Do not neglect to study the sacred text in each section, especially if you are familiar with it, because there is significance in the placement of the text and the revelation it provides.

There is a point where you as the reader realize this revelation and book is personal to Taquetta and Reenita, not just information. The practical methods she shares are a breath of fresh air, that lead you to experience real growth and transformation. The notion of dialoguing with yourself is genius in learning to covenant and stand inside the voice of God. The Word and VOICE of God is active on the pages of this book, so get ready, get ready, get ready, for divine encounters, as Holy Spirit leads you through an in-depth personal study of your heart and soul, so as to discern the voice of God more clearly for yourself and those you will release his word to.

Dana Wade
Blogger, Coach
Spirit-Filled Ministry & Life Coaching
dana@danawade.coach
www.DanaWade.coach

Table of Contents

Identifying Words of the Lord

Just because a word of revelation from God is spoken does not mean it is a prophecy. Prophecy, exhortation, the word of knowledge, the word of wisdom, tongues, interpretations of tongues and other verbal forms of edification are all vocal gifts. However, they are very distinct and separate operations of the Holy Spirit. To say every spoken word is "prophecy" is simply wrong.

It is important to know what type of word you are receiving from God and giving to the receiver so the word can be applied and governed applicably. This diminishes error with mishandling the word and with having expectations or perceptions of the word that God did not state. For this reason, I teach my team the types of words God provides, and encourage them to share what type of word it is when they are releasing it to others (***Study 1Corinthians 12 and Isaiah 11***).

Prophecy - Edify, comfort, and exhort a person or body of people; testifies of the goodness of Jesus. Though the releaser may provide past and present knowledge, the prophecy provides foresight into the future. If there is no foresight, it is not a prophecy. If a person is in the office of a prophet, they can judge, rebuke, correct, direct, display the anger of the Lord to a people, region, or nation.

*Prophecy in the Greek is **prophēteia** and means "prediction (scriptural or other), a discourse emanating from divine inspiration and declaring the purposes of God, whether by reproving and admonishing the wicked, or comforting the afflicted, or revealing things hidden; esp. by foretelling future events."*

1

Exhortation, Edification, Encouragement - An utterance, discourse, declaration, poem, affirmation, conversation, address, speech, prayer, teaching, conveying motivation, invitation, comfort, encouragement, strength, love, mercy, goodness, faithfulness, and spiritual help that SHIFT a person or atmosphere into the presence, focus, and purpose of God. A person with this gift operates through the sovereignty of God. They are clear and unwavering about his character and nature and are able to empower people to trust his sovereignty (*Acts 11:23-24, Acts 14:21-22, Acts 15:32, Romans 12:7-8, Romans 14:19 Romans 15:2, John 14:16, 2Timothy 4:2, 1Thessalonians 5:11*).

Exhortation in Greek *is parakaléō* meaning to properly, *"to call near, invite, invoke, intreat, make a call, summons, to encourage, urge, comfort, strengthen, or receive consolation."* Refers to believers offering up evidence that stands up in God's court where God's judgment and justice are used to empower a person, place, situation, or thing.

Edification in Greek is **oikodomé** which is *"the act of building, a building, spiritual advancement, edification or upbuilding."* A person is actually operating as a divine architecture to build a structure whether that be a person, place, or thing. It is the divine ability to promote growth in Godly wisdom, quality, honor, holiness, equity, joy, and fulfillment.

Encouragement in Greek is **paráklēsis** and *"it is an intimate call that someone personally gives to deliver God's verdict, the close-call that reveals how the Lord weighs in the relevant facts (evidence)."* It is a *"holy urging"* of the Lord directly motivating, empowering, supporting, prompting, and inspiring believers to carry out his plan and purpose in their lives and spheres of influence.

Knowledge- Facts, information, understanding, or the state of being aware of something about a person or situation via the Holy Spirit. One with this gift can also exemplify knowledge beyond their years or natural understanding. They have no means of proving what they know other than by the Holy Spirit and the confirmation of others. When they study information, they receive increased knowledge from the Holy Spirit even though they do not have the education or expertise for what they know. Such persons may also bring forth, report, make known, give facts, pass on, convey awareness, have insight, understanding, intelligence via the Holy Spirit. What they share is intended to draw the person into trusting God and posturing them in a place of receiving deliverance, healing, prophecy, and instruction to further advance their lives or situations through the purpose of God.

Knowledge in Greek is ***gnósis*** meaning *"knowledge, science, doctrine, intelligence, or divine understanding."* It is the knowledge of God offered to advance the gospel through what has been conveyed.

Wisdom - The natural and/or spiritual ability to understand things that other people cannot understand or do not have the knowledge of. They possess a perspective of what is proper, reasonable, good sense or balanced judgment. Those with the gift of wisdom have the experience, gift of common sense, enlightenment, clear thinking, foresight, perception, brains, sanity, or stability of God released to enlighten, empower, and advance people, situations, lands, atmospheres, and regions. The wisdom of God actually has a personality. *James 3:17* contends that *"But the wisdom that is from above is first pure, then peaceable, gentle, and easy to be intreated, full of mercy and good fruits, without partiality, and without hypocrisy."*

Wisdom in the Greek is **sophia** and means *"broad and full of intelligence, the intimate understanding of God's word and purpose."*

Proverbs 4:7 *Wisdom is the principal thing; therefore get wisdom: and with all thy getting get understanding.*

The word principal means chief, first, first fruits, order, rank, beginning. It is essential to receive wisdom from God before making any decisions and putting any actions in motion. Wisdom in the Hebrews is *hakma*, meaning skillful. It means skillful in:

1. War
2. Administration of wisdom
3. Religious affairs
4. Ethical matters

Wisdom enables a person to skillfully implement the will, intent, and purposes of God. People can receive advice, but if that insight does not reveal skill that enables a person to understand and activate what God is saying, then it is not God's wisdom.

Counsel – Insight that breathes life, instruction, exploration, direction, strategy, support, encouragement, focus, into a person or situation to help process and progress into them or that matter towards the destined purpose in God.

Counsel in Greek is **sumboulion** which is defined as *"a body of advisers (assessors) in a court, a council, consultation, counsel, advice; resolution, decree."*

Counseling is not advice. It is a committed processing to wholeness. The counselor or releaser of the word is not responsible for the healing, but is responsible for making

4

themselves available to the healing process. Words of counsel provide enlightenment and instruction of how to journey with God to a specific point of wellness. This counsel can have a prophetic element to a future destination, but the instruction and exploration itself is not prophecy. It is the counsel of the Lord.

Understanding - To perceive the meaning of, grasp the idea of, comprehend, connect the insights, or provide clarity to what God is speaking or what is being revealed. Understanding means to assign a meaning to, interpret; to comprehend the significance or importance of, to learn, perceive, hear, accept as true, trust or believe. It also means to embrace, partner with or grab hold to a thirst for knowledge, discern, sense, recognize, make sense of, fathom, or take in the truth, will, intent, and purpose of the wisdom and revelation that is being given.

Understand in Hebrew is ***binah*** meaning *"knowledge, wisdom, meaning, perfectly, understanding, discernment, and truth."*

Speaking in Tongues (*1Corinthians 14:4-5*) – Is the literal dialect and prayer language between you and God given to you by the Holy Spirit. Speaking in tongues is a real language. It is the voice of God is speaking through you in different languages that he desires to impart into your life.

Tongues in Greek is ***glóssa*** meaning *"a language that is not naturally acquired; a tongue, used of flowing speech, verbal utterance, speaking that is inspired by God."*

Interpretation of Tongues - Being able to translate what God is saying and speaking from one language to another where the people are able to understand his revelation, knowledge, word, counsel, strategy, guidance, and instruction. This gift tends to be released when there are prophetic words and prayer going forth. Someone may speak in tongues and SHIFT from speaking in tongues to praying or prophesying what the Lord is wanting to be said or desire to be released at that time. Some may also speak in tongues and another person/s may interpret what is said.

Strategy – A buzz word we tend to hear in this day and age is *"strategy."* We have come to recognize that as God speaks, we also need strategy to implement what he is saying. This is good because God's words tend to be progressive and requires movement and work along with faith to manifest them.

> *John 2:26 For as the body without the spirit is dead, so faith without works is dead also.*

Even if we are standing in faith, it requires energy, focus, and active contending to remain grounded in what God has said. This in and of itself may require strategy so that we do not give into unbelief, ungodly voices, or fatigue. We may need to be careful of being in certain places, being around certain people, remain fervent in fasting and praying, building ourselves up in a particular characteristic in God so we will not get sifted by the enemy or unholy alliances. Thus infers strategy.

Dictionary.com defines *strategy* as, *"the science or art of combining and employing the means of war in planning and directing large military movements and operations."* It is *"a plan, method, or series of maneuvers or stratagems for obtaining a specific goal or result."*

A strategy can include words of exhortation, wisdom, revelation, knowledge, counsel, and understanding. All of these can be part of your strategy. A strategy is your war plan that keeps us fortified as we walk out the words of God. Once you have the strategy, then you implement tactics necessary to SHIFT forward in unveiling the word God has given you.

Strategy Keeps You:

Offensive against attacks	Grounded
Rooted	Focused
Seated in heavenly places of authority	Towering over trials & obstacles

Strategy Provides:

Shelter	Protection
Trust	Hope
Fortress	Defense
Deliverance	Rescue
Recovery	Healing
Peace despite war	Rest from war
Safety for harvest & spoils of war	Set altar of worship

Strategy helps you to resist being worried, fearful, inferior, insecure as you know God's got you. He has given you a plan to keep you solidified in his secret place. You can work your strategy to remain fortified as God works his word for and in you. You do not change the strategy unless God leads. I seek God for strategy as weeks, months, and seasons change so I will know how to further progress in a word or vision that God is given me. I do this because what may have worked last week or month may not work for this week or month. I may be facing different devils, trials, obstacles and require a different strategy. I will only know that by seeking God for that revelation. I implement what God says, and if he does not give me anything, then I continue to work the current strategy he has provided.

Study Exploration

1. As God releases words to you, identify with him what type of word it is. Make sure you label it as such when journaling it or when sharing it with others. The more you identify your well, the more mature you will become in knowing how God speaks, hearing him, and being able to convey his word to others.

2. As God would release words, seek him for a strategy for how to stand and birth forth what he is speaking. Do not sway from the strategy unless he releases another strategy. When you find yourself fearful, weary, or stressed, check your strategy to make sure you are implementing it properly. Sometimes we are not implementing the full strategy, and it can cause sifting or unnecessary warfare. God may tell you to declare the prophetic word out loud three times a day for a week and to fast and pray until 5pm. You may fast and pray but not declare three times a day and thus ensue sifting and warfare. You may think this part is unnecessary, forget to do it, or just lax. But when reassessing your strategy, you will remember to implement this part, and it will stop the sifting and unnecessary warfare. So always go back and reassess and do everything God is requiring, even those things you may think are meaningless. God uses the foolish things to confound the wise. Be mindful of that and know your strategy has power to fortify you against the enemy.

> *2Corinthians 1:27 But God hath chosen the foolish things of the world to confound the wise; and God hath chosen the weak things of the world to confound the things which are mighty.*
>
> *2Corinthians 10:4 For the weapons of our warfare are not carnal, but mighty through God to the pulling down of strong holds.* **SHIFT!**

Posture To Hear

We are quick to see or hear a word and contend that word is of the Lord. In a day and age where "prophecy" is being released so loosely, I had to examine whether we really know how to discern God's voice from our own, others, witchcraft, or the devil. In all my years of attending prophetic training, I have never been taught this. I have been taught to bubble up and speak the first thing that comes to my spirit. Yet, *1John 4* says try every spirit to see if it be of God.

> *1John 4:1 Beloved, believe not every spirit, but try the spirits whether they are of God: because many false prophets are gone out into the world.*

When we try the word, many become defensive. Generally, because we tend to test a word by whether it benefits us, agrees with our needs, desires, and what we deem to be our convictions, than a true testing of whether it is of God. Such a posture causes us to agree with words that have no real power to SHIFT us anywhere in God, clogs and entangles us in activities and behaviors to try and make the word be God, and blocks his true word from coming to pass. The devil, witches, and emotions of people are sounding like God every day, but how much time do we spend working that word before we realize it may not be God???

Journal your thoughts as you study this passage of scripture and consider the words that are in bold. Journal regarding which areas you need to mature in as you explore the passage of scripture.

> *Habakkuk 2:1-2 The Amplified Bible [OH, I know, I have been rash to talk out plainly this way to God!] I will [in my thinking] stand upon my post of observation and station*

9

*myself on the tower or fortress, and will **watch** to see what He will say within me and **what answer I will make** [as His mouthpiece] to the perplexities of my complaint against Him. And the Lord answered me and said, **Write the vision** and **engrave** it so plainly upon tablets that everyone who passes may [be able to] read [it easily and quickly] as he **hastens** by.*

Journal Notes:

_____

_____

_____

_____

_____

_____

_____

_____

_____

_____

_____

_____

_____

_____

_____

_____

_____

_____

_____

_____

_____

_____

Ask God how important each of the words are to posturing yourself to hear his voice.

- Stand

  _____
  _____
  _____
  _____
  _____
  _____
  _____
  _____

- Station

  _____
  _____
  _____
  _____
  _____
  _____
  _____

- Watch

  _____
  _____
  _____
  _____
  _____
  _____
  _____
  _____

- Answer

  _____
  _____
  _____
  _____
  _____
  _____
  _____

- Engrave

  _____
  _____
  _____
  _____
  _____
  _____

- Hasten

  _____
  _____
  _____
  _____
  _____

Still Small Voice
Written By: Minister Nina Cook & Minister Reenita Keys of Kingdom Shifters Ministries

God's Voice is often spoken in the stillness.

1Kings 19:11-12 And he said, Go forth, and stand upon the mount before the Lord. And, behold, the Lord passed by, and a great and strong wind rent the mountains, and brake in pieces the rocks before the Lord; but the Lord was not in the wind: and after the wind an earthquake; but the Lord was not in the earthquake: And after the earthquake a fire; but the Lord was not in the fire: and after the fire a still small voice.

Psalm 46:10 says, "Be still, and know that I am God."

Still is *rapa* in the Hebrew and means:
1. abate, cease, consume, draw
2. faint, be wax feeble, fail, faint
3. idle, leave, let alone, slack, stay, be still,
4. be slothful, weaken, sink down, sink, relax

Take some time and meditate on those words with the Lord and journal what it truly means to be still and listen for God's still voice.

_____

_____

_____

_____

_____

_____

_____

_____

_____

_____

_____

_____

_____

_____

God loves relationship, covenant, and intimacy. He speaks to us in his "STILL, small voice." It is in stillness, not busyness, that we tune our spiritual ears to hear the voice of God. At times, his voice can be drowned out amid all the challenges, busyness, demands, needs, and desires of our daily lives. God speaks in the stillness to draw us into intentionality with hearing and communing with him. He wants to make sure we deem it important to press into his presence to learn his voice, spend time with him, and to hear from him. He teaches us about him by creating an atmosphere and experience where we have to become

- dead like
- feeble like a baby
- weakened and reliant on him
- faint with surrender
- sunk in, chill
- drawn to his spirit

Speaking in a still voice produces distinction and notability to God's voice that enables us to discern his voice from other voices in our lives. It trains us to discern his voice from the voice of our soul, the world, the devil, and any other voice that is not of him. It boasts of how we have spent time in intimacy training and tuning our ear to hear him, to know him, to love him, to love what he speaks, and to live by what he speaks.

A child knows the voice of their mother or father. They know their voices from any other voice because the parents spent time speaking to them while they were in the womb. Babies can listen but cannot see very well when they are born. They still recognize the voice of their mother and father because of the time spent with them in the womb and in the nurturing process of development. When we are saved, we go through a rebirthing of becoming anew in our restored relationship with the Lord. He knew us before our mother's womb and knitted us there (*Psalms 139:9*). The fall of man brought division between us and his voice, but Jesus redeemed us where we can now spend time in our baby stage of birthing, learning his voice, and then maturing to living by his voice. The more time spent with God, the more discerning we are in detecting his still voice regardless of how busy, loud, and chaotic life becomes. The covenant we develop in intimacy becomes the reality of what guides us every day of our life as we are dependent, in love, and guided by "GOD'S STILL SMALL VOICE!

Aside from normal everyday prayer, spend 15 minutes a day in silence listening for God's still small voice. Journal what he says. Do this consistently so you can become feeble to always hearing and living by his still small voice. SHIFT!

Know Them Scriptures

We are to meditate and study the scriptures as this helps us discern God's voice. God's voice aligns with his scriptures and the fruit of who he is. There are no biases, bigotry, double dealings, sin, or soulish dipping with the biblical word of God. His scriptures – his standards are never changing. They remain the same and confirm the truth of his voice.

Meditate on each scripture and ask God for revelation of how each one is important to knowing him through his word.

> **Psalms 1:1-2** *Blessed is the man that walketh not in the counsel of the ungodly, nor standeth in the way of sinners, nor sitteth in the seat of the scornful. But his delight is in the law of the Lord; and in his law doth he meditate day and night.*

> **Psalms 63:6** *On my bed I remember you; I think of you through the watches of the night.*

> **Psalms 119:15** *I meditate on your precepts and consider your ways.*

> **Psalms 119:97-99** *Oh, how I love your law! I meditate on it all day long. Your commands are always with me and make me wiser than my enemies. I have more insight than all my teachers, for I meditate on your statutes.*

> **Proverbs 4:20-22** *My son, pay attention to what I say; turn your ear to my words. Do not let them out of your sight, keep them within your heart; for they are life to those who find them and health to one's whole body.*

2Timothy 2:15 Study to shew thyself approved unto God, a workman that needeth not to be ashamed, rightly dividing the word of truth.

Hebrews 13:8 Jesus Christ is the same yesterday, today, and forever.

1Peter 1:25 But the word of the Lord endureth for ever. And this is the word which by the gospel is preached unto you.

The more you study your bible, the more it becomes the identity of you, while teaching you about the character and nature of God. There is a difference between the scriptures confirming what is being spoken and you choosing a scripture or twisting a scripture to align with a word you have received. The key is motive and making sure God is guiding you to confirmation, and you are not using witchcraft manipulations to align scripture to the word. Also, be mindful not to use a scripture out of context or like magic because you open the door to trickery. Ask the Holy Spirit to guide you to a scripture to confirm a word. You can look up scriptures related to a word you receive but make sure you ask God for further revelation so you will know what he is saying and if that scripture applies. Timing is also important so as you are receiving biblical confirmation, ask God for the time and season of operating in that word and be guided by his leading.

The Knower Of God

God speaks through our knower - this is where you just know wisdoms, truths, standards, rights and wrongs, character, nature, and God's will, without having any emotions, physical signs, or confirmation from any outside force. God created us so his knower is in us.

> *Romans 1:19-21 The Amplified Bible For that which is known about God is evident to them and made plain in their inner consciousness, because God [Himself] has shown it to them. For ever since the creation of the world His invisible nature and attributes, that is, His eternal power and divinity, have been made intelligible and clearly discernible in and through the things that have been made (His handiworks). So [men] are without excuse [altogether without any defense or justification], Because when they knew and recognized Him as God, they did not honor and glorify Him as God or give Him thanks. But instead they became futile and godless in their thinking [with vain imaginings, foolish reasoning, and stupid speculations] and their senseless minds were darkened.*

- There are things we will just know about God because he put it in us to know him and to know them.
- We can reject them, but we know them regardless.
- We can choose our own will, but we know his will regardless.
- We can become reprobate to them and even deject the outward manifestations of God, but we know regardless.

Many people mistake the knower for intuition (keen and quick insight) or Dejavu (tedious familiarity, feelings of having already experienced the present situation). These tend to operate through our minds, emotions or natural senses. Our knower operates through our spirit. Spirit to spirit is where we commune and converse with God.

It is the spirit of God quickening our faith to know by faith and not by sight; you know God, know his will and purpose, and know he is with you even though you cannot naturally trace him or feel him. This is a very important posture of maturity for the believer to attain because we are so emotion and sign driven. Though our flesh and emotions feel God, he is a spirit. We must know him by the spirit, engage him by the spirit, and be guided by our spirit. Emotions and signs can mislead us, but God's spirit is always pure and accurate. That is the reason David wanted a clean heart and a right spirit.

> *Psalms 51:10* *Create in me a clean heart, O God; and renew a right spirit within me.*

He knew God's spirit would guide him correctly. There will be seasons in your spiritual walk when all you will have is your knower to guide you. You will not feel God. You will not hear God. But you will know he is leading and guiding you. You will have a strong stance of the knower in you and will not be able to explain the reason you know what you know, but you will have a strong unwavering stance in God. This may stress and confuse some of you because it is an unfamiliar and uncomfortable place. But God takes us through these seasons to mature our faith in him. He also allows these seasons when he has taken us through a season of learning and it is time to activate what we have learned. Apostles and prophets have frequent seasons of the knower. The knower is part of the prophets' mantle. Apostles and prophets tend to embody the very essence of God where they go in his stead to speak and complete the work of the kingdom. They will only have a measure of what he desires to do on an assignment or have a knowing that they are to go. But not much else aside from that. God will have them operating in the knower so they can be totally reliant upon him, such that when they open their mouth to speak, it is his literal word and revelation coming forth.

> **Psalms 81:10** *I am the LORD thy God, which brought thee out of the land of Egypt: open thy mouth wide, and I will fill it.*

In the season of the knower, it is important to consecrate yourself and keep yourself submitted before God so you operate through a pure well. Otherwise, you will have character challenges of inadequacy, insecurity, and being frustrated with those you are releasing the words too, especially if they are inconsistent with trusting the Lord, and the revelation he is giving you to lead them to victory.

Study Exploration
1. Study the story of Moses and journal what you learned as he battled operating in the knower. Journal a strategy for how you can avoid making the mistakes he made.
2. Journal experiences you have had with seasons of the knower. Repent for any ways you did not handle those seasons properly. Study scriptures on areas you need to mature your character for future seasons of the knower. Journal a consecration plan you can implement to help you be successful during future knower seasons.
3. Study **Romans 8** and ask God for revelation concerning hearing his voice over flesh and emotions.

Spiritual Senses

God speaks through our spiritual senses. When reading *Isaiah 6:1-8*, we find Isaiah experiencing a vision where all his senses were enthralled.

> *Isaiah 6:1-8 In the year that king Uzziah died I saw (**spiritually seeing**) also the Lord sitting upon a throne, high and lifted up, and his train filled the temple. Above it stood the seraphims: each one had six wings; with twain he covered his face, and with twain he covered his feet, and with twain he did fly. And one cried unto another, and said, Holy, holy, holy, is the Lord of hosts: the whole earth is full of his glory. And the posts of the door moved at the voice of him that cried, and the house was filled with smoke (**spiritually smelling and seeing**).*
>
> *Then said I, Woe is me! for I am undone; because I am a man of unclean lips, and I dwell in the midst of a people of unclean lips: for mine eyes have seen the King, the Lord of hosts (**spiritually perceiving his state and the state of the people**). Then flew one of the seraphims unto me, having a live coal in his hand, which he had taken with the tongs from off the altar: And he laid it upon my mouth (**spiritual touch and spiritual taste**), and said, Lo, this hath touched thy lips; and thine iniquity is taken away, and thy sin purged. Also I heard (**spiritually hearing**) the voice of the Lord, saying, Whom shall I send, and who will go for us? Then said I, Here am I; send me.*

You may or may not literally experience sensation through your natural senses, but please understand that what is being spoken by God to you is released to and through your spirit - the senses of the Holy Spirit in you.

You discern through your senses in the following ways:

- Seeing - eyes
- Hearing - ears
- Smelling - nose
- Tasting - mouth
- Touching - feeling, impression, sensation, physical awareness
- Perceiving - sensing, having a conscious awareness, sensation or recognition of something

Seeing

> **Psalms 36:9** *For with thee is the fountain of life: in thy light shall we see light.*

> **Ephesians 1** *The eyes of your understanding being enlightened; that ye may know what is the hope of his calling, and what the riches of the glory of his inheritance in the saints, And what is the exceeding greatness of his power to us-ward who believe, according to the working of his mighty power*

> **Mark 8:17-18** *Now the disciples had forgotten to take bread, neither had they in the ship with them more than one loaf. And he charged them, saying, Take heed, beware of the leaven of the Pharisees, and of the leaven of Herod. And they reasoned among themselves, saying, It is because we have no bread. And when Jesus knew it, he saith unto them, Why reason ye, because ye have no bread? perceive ye not yet, neither understand? have ye your heart yet hardened? Having eyes, see ye not? and having ears, hear ye not? and do ye not remember?*

Though there are vain imaginations that should be cast down, there are also spiritual imaginations placed in our spirit by the Lord. Our spiritual imaginations are weapons against the enemy that keep us delivered and aligned with the truth and will of the Lord.

> **2Corinthians 10:4-5** *(For the weapons of our warfare are not carnal, but mighty through God to the pulling down of strong holds;) Casting down imaginations, and every high thing that exalteth itself against the knowledge of God, and bringing into captivity every thought to the obedience of Christ.*

Hearing

> **Romans 10:17** *So then faith cometh by hearing, and hearing by the word of God.*

> **Job 42:5** *I have heard of thee by the hearing of the ear: but now mine eye seeth thee.*

> **John 10:27 The Amplified Bible** *The sheep that are My own hear and are listening to My voice; and I know them, and they follow Me.*

> **Isaiah 55:3** *Incline your ear and come to Me Listen, that you may live; And I will make an everlasting covenant with you, According to the faithful mercies shown to David.*

> **1Kings 19:11-13** *Then He said, "Go out, and stand on the mountain before the Lord." And behold, the Lord passed by, and a great and strong wind tore into the mountains and broke the rocks in pieces before the Lord, but the Lord was not in the wind; and after the wind an earthquake, but the Lord was not in the earthquake; and after the earthquake a fire, but the Lord was not in the fire; and after the fire a still small voice. So it was, when Elijah heard it, that he wrapped his face in his mantle and went out and stood in the entrance of*

the cave. Suddenly a voice came to him, and said, "What are you doing here, Elijah?"

Though we can hear God with our natural ears, it is our spirit that should be tuned in to hear God. Our spirit should be postured to listen attentively to learn and discern God's voice, and to have unwavering faith in what he is speaking.

Smelling

Proverbs 16:24 *Pleasant words are as an honeycomb, sweet to the soul, and health to the bones.*

Song of Songs 1:12 *While the king sitteth at his table, my spikenard sendeth forth the smell thereof.*

2Corinthians 2:15 *For we are a fragrance of Christ to God among those who are being saved and among those who are perishing.*

Ephesians 5:1-2 *Therefore be imitators of God, as beloved children; and walk in love, just as Christ also loved you and gave Himself up for us, an offering and a sacrifice to God as a fragrant aroma.*

Proverbs 27:9 *Oil and perfume make the heart glad, So a man's counsel is sweet to his friend.*

Hosea 14:6 *His shoots will sprout, And his beauty will be like the olive tree And his fragrance like the cedars of Lebanon.*

Philippians 4:18 *But I have all, and abound: I am full, having received of Epaphroditus the things which were sent from you, an odour of a sweet smell, a sacrifice acceptable, well pleasing to God.*

The spiritual ability to smell the essence of God, heaven, and his kingdom is probably our most undeveloped spiritual sense. We can smell devils, witchcraft, sin, and strange fire, but rarely do we discern the aroma of God. I would contend that because of this, we miss out on a lot of spiritual encounters with God, learning his fragrance, and receiving words through this well. Ask God to develop your spiritual sense of smell and to make you aware of his fragrances and smells in general as he releases his words and divine encounters to you.

Tasting

> *Psalms 34:8 O taste and see that the Lord is good: blessed is the man that trusteth in him.*

> *Psalms 66:17-18 I cried unto him with my mouth, and he was extolled with my tongue. If I regard iniquity in my heart, the Lord will not hear me:*

> *Job 6:30 Is there iniquity in my tongue? cannot my taste discern perverse things?*

> *Psalms 119:103 How sweet are thy words unto my taste! yea, sweeter than honey to my mouth!*

> *Matthew 4:4 And he answered and said, it is written, Man shall not live by bread alone, but by every word that proceedeth out of the mouth of God.*

> *Song of Solomon 2:3 As the apple tree among the trees of the wood, so is my beloved among the sons. I sat down under his shadow with great delight, and his fruit was sweet to my taste.*

John 8:52 Then said the Jews unto him, Now we know that thou hast a devil. Abraham is dead, and the prophets; and thou sayest, If a man keep my saying, he shall never taste (nourish on) of death.

Sometimes the spiritual manna and words of God are delicious; sometimes they are bitter, but all are for our good. Isaiah had coal placed upon his tongue. That could not have tasted or felt good, but it purified his mouth. How many of us would have spirit tasted that and discerned it as God? Like me, some of you probably would have assumed it was a demon flying in trying to disrupt your divine moment with the Lord. But spiritually maturing our sense of taste, will enable us to discern the taste and manna of the Lord.

Touching

Jeremiah 1:9 Then the Lord put forth his hand, and touched my mouth. And the Lord said unto me, Behold, I have put my words in thy mouth.

Hebrews 4:15 For we have not an high priest which cannot be touched with the feeling of our infirmities; but was in all points tempted like as we are, yet without sin.

Daniel 10:10 And, behold, an hand touched me, which set me upon my knees and upon the palms of my hands.

Matthew 14:36 And besought him that they might only touch the hem of his garment: and as many as touched were made perfectly whole.

Matthew 20:34 So Jesus had compassion on them, and touched their eyes: and immediately their eyes received sight, and they followed him.

We may assume that everything we physically feel when praying, in a service, or communing, and inquiring of God is of him. Though our natural flesh can feel and experience him, we should be feeling the touch of God through our spirit. This is where we truly know we encountered God and was truly transformed by touching him. When the woman with the issue of blood touched the hem of Jesus' garment, he did not say *who touched my hem?* No, he said, *who touched me?* He did not refer to his hem because the touch he experienced was from spirit to spirit. It was so spiritual that virtue left him — he felt the miracle leave him.

> *Luke 8:45-48 And Jesus said, Who touched me? When all denied, Peter and they that were with him said, Master, the multitude throng thee and press thee, and sayest thou, Who touched me? And Jesus said, Somebody hath touched me: for I perceive that virtue is gone out of me. And when the woman saw that she was not hid, she came trembling, and falling down before him, she declared unto him before all the people for what cause she had touched him, and how she was healed immediately. And he said unto her, Daughter, be of good comfort: thy faith hath made thee whole; go in peace.*

Jesus felt this encounter in his spirit while others were physically thronging him. People were physically bumping up against Jesus and did not feel a thing. That word *"press"* means to squeeze like grapes, so this was a pressing on every side. The disciples were the closest to him and were probably bumping up against him the most, yet they were challenged that he would make such an inquiry. They were touching him physically but not spiritually. The woman with the issue of blood delivered a touch through her spirit. Physically, it was the hem of his garment, spiritually, it pierced his spirit. Jesus' spirit responded as she was physically healed. We can be in God's presence and get all kind of goosebumps, raised hairs, quickening, tingling sensations, drunken feelings, drug-like highs, orgasmic emotional and physical sensations, and though these things are not always or all bad, his true spiritual touch is determined by transformation. Did virtue leave him and change you? Did a download of revelation infuse you? Did you just touch him physically or did you TOUCH him spiritually?

Getting caught up in physical touch and how "God feels" can hinder our ability to have true spiritual encounters with his touch. It is okay to enjoy the physical touches, but be intentional to spiritually mature your sense of spiritual touch - posture your spirit to touch him. SHIFT!

Study Exploration
1. What is the difference between spiritual and natural senses?
2. How would you know if you were hearing God through your spiritual or natural senses?
3. Journal the spiritual senses God uses the most to speak to you. It is important to know this so you can be more cognizant of seeking these wells to hear him.
4. Journal the wells of your senses that you need to mature. Take a week to practice hearing God through that well. Journal your experiences.
5. Use three of your prophetic words, dreams, or spiritual visitations to identify how God spoke through your spiritual senses.
6. As you have encounters with God in the future, be mindful of how he is engaging you through your senses, even during prayer and praise and worship. Journal these experiences and reference what he is speaking or what you are sensing spiritually. This will increase your keenness in being able to spiritually sense and connect with him through these spiritual wells. **SHIFT!**

The Spiritual Power Of God's Words

Most often we mistake the voice of the Lord for our own thoughts as God tends to speak through our spirit from his Spirit.

> *John 4:24 says, God is a Spirit: and they that worship him must worship him in spirit and in truth.*

This scripture is revealing that communication with God is Spirit to Spirit, not brain to brain, thoughts to thoughts, heart to heart, soul to soul, emotions to emotions, or mouth to ear, which are the ways we can communicate and speak with ourselves and to one another in the natural realm.

Though God has a heart, mind, thoughts, and emotions, and we can know and have these parts of him, *John 4:24* lets us know that he communes with us from Spirit to Spirit. We ask for and take on these factors of his identity, character, and nature, but we commune and converse through our Spirit to Spirit interactions with him.

Decree each scripture out loud three times and then spend ten minutes just resting in the presence of God and allowing him to further transform you in the scriptures. Journal any significant encounters of transformation you notice. After that, continue on with reading this chapter.

> *Philippians 2:5 Let this mind be in you, which was also in Christ Jesus.*

> *Romans 12:2 And be not conformed to this world: but be ye transformed by the renewing of your mind, that ye may prove what is that good, and acceptable, and perfect, will of God.*

1Corinthians 2:16 *For who hath known the mind of the Lord, that he may instruct him? But we have the mind of Christ.*

1Peter 1:13 *Wherefore gird up the loins of your mind, be sober, and hope to the end for the grace that is to be brought unto you at the revelation of Jesus Christ;*

Romans 8:1 *[There is] therefore now no condemnation to them which are in Christ Jesus, who walk not after the flesh, but after the Spirit.*

Philippians 4:8 *Finally, brethren, whatsoever things are true, whatsoever things [are] honest, whatsoever things [are] just, whatsoever things [are] pure, whatsoever things [are] lovely, whatsoever things [are] of good report; if [there be] any virtue, and if [there be] any praise, think on these things.*

Jeremiah 29:11 *For I know the thoughts I think toward you, says the Lord, thoughts of peace and not of evil, to give you a future and a hope.*

Psalms 139:16-17 *Your eyes saw my substance, being yet unformed. And in Your book they all were written, the days fashioned for me, when as yet there were none of them. How precious also are Your thoughts to me, O God! How great is the sum of them!*

Romans 12:2 *Do not conform to the pattern of this world, but be transformed by the renewing of your mind. Then you will be able to test and approve what God's will is – his good, pleasing and perfect will.*

Psalms 51:10 *Create in me a pure heart, O God, and renew a steadfast spirit within me.*

Ezekiel 36:26 A new heart also will I give you, and a new spirit will I put within you: and I will take away the stony heart out of your flesh, and I will give you an heart of flesh.

Though we take on his essence, the Lord speaks to our spirits through thoughts and impressions that are from his spirit to our spirit. As we mature in his essence – his heart, mind, thoughts, and emotions – we take on his identity which helps us identify his voice quickly and keenly and embody what he is speaking. It is also the reason we assume that God's voice sounds like our voice. We are actually being unveiled from glory to glory in the identity of God – of his likeness that we were to have at the beginning of mankind. This is a great endeavor as we should be becoming more like him, but we still need to know that his thoughts are his and not ours and are higher than our thoughts, and that his thoughts are being spoken from his spirit to our spirit.

Isaiah 55:8-9 For my thoughts are not your thoughts, neither are your ways my ways, declares the Lord. As the heavens are higher than the earth, so are my ways higher than your ways and my thoughts than your thoughts.

I want to zone in on this point so it becomes the truth of what we understand about God. Through communing with him, we can know his voice. His thoughts are never beyond our reach, however, God's voice is always higher than ours, and it is from his spirit to our spirit that we hear him.

Thoughts is **machashebeth** in the Hebrew and means:
1. a contrivance, i.e. (concretely) a texture, machine, or (abstractly) intention
2. plan (whether bad, a plot; or good, advice)
3. cunning (work), curious work, device(-sed), imagination
4. thought, device, plan, purpose, invention, invented

This is where the power and substance of what God is speaking comes from as his words are literal machines and inventions that carry his creative plans and purposes. Words create. They either create what God is speaking, or they create what we are speaking. If they are not God's words but are spoken as if they are his words, then they are not creating his inventions, his plans, or his purposes. This is the reason we are to have spirit to spirit relationship and encounters with him. We do not want to invent something that he is not saying, or lead people to believe or pursue something he is not saying.

Our minds, souls, hearts, and emotions can create something that could very well lead others astray. In *Exodus 32*, the Israelites had the word of the Lord about the promise land and all they would receive when they got there.

> *Exodus 3:17 And I have said, I will bring you up out of the affliction of Egypt unto the land of the Canaanites, and the Hittites, and the Amorites, and the Perizzites, and the Hivites, and the Jebusites, unto a land flowing with milk and honey.*

This was a prophetic promise that had been leading their journey and God had been demonstrating himself miraculously on their behalf. Moses had gone into the mountains to commune with God and they became restless in thinking he was not going to return and talked Aaron into making them a golded calf – an idol God.

> *Exodus 32:1-5 And when the people saw that Moses delayed to come down out of the mount, the people gathered themselves together unto Aaron, and said unto him, Up, make us gods, which shall go before us; for as for this Moses, the man that brought us up out of the land of Egypt, we wot*

not what is become of him. And Aaron said unto them, Break off the golden earrings, which are in the ears of your wives, of your sons, and of your daughters, and bring them unto me. And all the people brake off the golden earrings which were in their ears, and brought them unto Aaron. And he received them at their hand, and fashioned it with a graving tool, after he had made it a molten calf: and they said, These be thy gods, O Israel, which brought thee up out of the land of Egypt. And when Aaron saw it, he built an altar before it; and Aaron made proclamation, and said, To morrow is a feast to the Lord.

The Bible says Moses was delayed. The Israelites nor Aaron did not think to go look for Moses. We can use our sanctified imagination and assume that they thought he had died, left them, or was not returning. No one thought to say, *"let's just wait a little while longer"* or even to say, *"let's go look for Moses."* The people had been enslaved in Egypt. They had endured hard labor and their souls were traumatized. They had unresolved issues from their bondage to slavery, and had idolatry in their minds, hearts, and souls from living around it. It had become ideology in their imagination even though they had been generationally conditioned to rely on the one true and living God. Instead of seeking God for what to do, meditating on the prophetic word they received about the promise land, and strengthening themselves in the Lord, they listened to their own voice – the voice of their minds, hearts, and souls, and decided to encourage Aaron to make them a golden calf. They told Aaron *"make us gods."* WOW! Even though they had a miraculous God who had delivered them from Egypt, personally journeyed with them, provided for them, gave them a cloud by day and fire by night, they wanted to create – INVENT – their own God so it could lead them. WOW! Aaron had them gather their golden earrings from their ears – their hearing – someone else can preach that

– and he fashioned them a golden calf. He was so pleased with himself that he made proclamations – got his preach on as he gazed upon his work and planned a celebration feast to further sacrifice unto the golden calf.

This invention was not from the spirit of God. It was from the heart of man. To them, it appeared to be a good idea and was fulfilling what they deemed to be an urgent need, but it was idolatry. All of this stemmed from the power of persuasive words as words have power. **Proverbs 18:21** says, *'Death and life are in the power of the tongue: and they that love it shall eat the fruit thereof.'*

- We have power to speak life or to speak death.
- We have power to create life or create death.
- We have power to release life or release death.

The Israelites thought they were creating life but they were inventing death. This is the reason we must watch what we speak and be guided only by the words that are coming from our spirit – from God's spirit to ours. If the Israelites would have stayed in tune with what God had spoken, it would not have mattered if Moses came back or not. God's prophetic word would have continued to guide them to the promise land. It had already been spoken and set out to do just what God intended, which was to SHIFT them into a land flowing with milk and honey.

Though God's thoughts are not our thoughts, neither are our ways his ways. God's ways represent his methods, mode of action, pathways, journeys, character, habits, plans, and purposes. They are not like ours, but they are not unattainable. We are to be pursuing his ways so we can come into covenant with what he desires for our lives. If you study the book of Exodus, you will find that the Israelites had a difficult time SHIFTING into relationship with God. He was the God of their fathers, and they were acquainted with him and how to worship him but did not seem to have personal covenant just yet. The entire journey to the promise land was about SHIFTING them into covenant relationship with God. The Israelites however, feared God, so they only wanted to speak to him through Moses. This is the reason they were so quick to make a golden calf when Moses was delayed. Personal relationship is what provokes you to rely on the pure voice of God. You cannot know God through your ancestors, immediate family, pastor, mentor, or friends. You have to know him for yourself. Only then can you know the power of his voice. Only then can you understand a spirit to spirit covenant connection with him.

The word *spirit* is **pnuema** in the Greek and means "breath." Our relationship with God, is from breath to breath. Breathing is essential for life and vitality. When you are not breathing you are DEAD. When you are not living by the spirit of God – breath to breath in him – you are spiritually DEAD. Relationship with him is life, and his voice creates life. I decree that you are grasping the power of this revelation even now. And that it is SHIFTING you only to want to live and breath from spirit to spirit with God. **SHIFT!**

Study Exploration
1. What does it mean to have a spirit to spirit relationship with God?
2. Spend time daily developing a spirit to spirit relationship with him and hearing him from this posture until it becomes a lifestyle and you commune with him all day every day, and hear him all throughout the day.
3. Ask God questions throughout the day and invite him into moments of your day so you can develop a spiritual ear to hear him even when you are not in your personal prayer

time. Focus on communing as a lifestyle where you walk breath to breath with him. Where you laugh with him, cry with him, share jokes with him, laugh with him, and hear him laugh and joke. Work on developing a relationship where you know him as your very own breath.

4. Journal what his voice sounds like in different seasons of your life (i.e., warfare, rest, harvest, planting, plowing, building, tiredness, sin, correction). Be sensitive to what his voice sounds like and how he speaks to you. This helps you to learn his character and his nature and how to know and receive him even when he is speaking rebuke, warnings, or something you may not want to hear.

Our Voice Versus God's Voice: Creature Versus the Creator

As we search out words we receive, we must know whether the word is being served from God or the devil - the creature or the Creator?

> **Romans 1:22-26** *Professing themselves to be wise, they became fools, And changed the glory of the uncorruptible God into an image made like to corruptible man, and to birds, and fourfooted beasts, and creeping things. Wherefore God also gave them up to uncleanness through the lusts of their own hearts, to dishonour their own bodies between themselves: Who changed the truth of God into a lie, and worshipped and served the creature more than the Creator, who is blessed for ever. Amen. For this cause God gave them up unto vile affections: for even their women did change the natural use into that which is against nature.*

Many equate this scripture to homosexuality but God is speaking about any sin that has become our God. It is very important to search and ask ourselves if the word we heard was a lust of our hearts, or really the word of the Lord. It is important to have that level of truth and conversation with ourselves and with God, such that we are not turned over to think that what we hear is really the will of God for us. It very well could be us becoming our own idols.

> **Proverbs 19:21 New International Translation** Many are the plans in a person's heart, but it is the LORD's purpose that prevails.

> **Jeremiah 17:7-11** *Blessed is the man that trusteth in the Lord, and whose hope the Lord is. For he shall be as a tree planted by the waters, and that spreadeth out her roots by the*

river, and shall not see when heat cometh, but her leaf shall be green; and shall not be careful in the year of drought, neither shall cease from yielding fruit. The heart is deceitful above all things, and desperately wicked: who can know it? I the Lord search the heart, I try the reins, even to give every man according to his ways, and according to the fruit of his doings. As the partridge sitteth on eggs, and hatcheth them not; so he that getteth riches, and not by right, shall leave them in the midst of his days, and at his end shall be a fool.

Matthew 6:20-24 *The Amplified Bible But gather and heap up and store for yourselves treasures in heaven, where neither moth nor rust nor worm consume and destroy, and where thieves do not break through and steal; For where your treasure is, there will your heart be also. The eye is the lamp of the body. So if your eye is sound, your entire body will be full of light. But if your eye is unsound, your whole body will be full of darkness. If then the very light in you [your conscience] is darkened, how dense is that darkness! No one can serve two masters; for either he will hate the one and love the other, or he will stand by and be devoted to the one and despise and be against the other. You cannot serve God and mammon (deceitful riches, money, possessions, or whatever is trusted in).*

Proverbs 4:23 *Keep thy heart with all diligence; for out of it are the issues of life.*

Our heart can also get entangled with the cares of life and become polluted by them. We must constantly keep our heart and seek to have the heart of God, otherwise it will begin to speak things that are of our will and not God's.

Be open to asking God if it is you or him speaking. Also, be conscious of your heart issues. Cleanse and heal from them and do not be quick to make decisions when you know your heart is not in a pure and diligent place with God. Journal words you may hear and wait until your heart is healthy to act on them, along with receiving confirmation of what has been spoken. If it is a now word, seek a mature accountability partner that can keep you balanced and accountable as you walk out the word and as you seek further healing of issues that could hinder the word. An accountability partner is not your best friend who you may or may not listen to. An accountability partner is a spiritual advisor that has God's best interest for you at heart. This person needs to be someone who will not be swayed by emotions or desires they may have for you or that you have for yourself.

Do not go on a wild goose chase for confirmation as this opens doors for the enemy to put signs, soul and heart pleasers, and angels of light in your path. Or you end up mistaking assumptions or happenstance for confirmations. Ask God to send confirmation and wait for him.

> *Philippians 4:6-7 New King James Version Be anxious for nothing, but in everything by prayer and supplication, with thanksgiving, let your requests be made known to God; and the peace of God, which surpasses all understanding, will guard your hearts and minds through Christ Jesus.*

When we are anxious, we can become troubled with cares, restless, unstable, stressed, seek to promote our own interests, and consumed with worry and anticipation. The word has exalted itself above God in our lives where we worship and idolize it and its' fulfillment rather than God.

If you are experiencing any of this when examining a word, then it is time to restore your posture of worship, love, and surrender to the Lord. Let him heal and rebalance you, then let him guide you into further insight about whether a word is from him or not. He will guide you into all truth. When this is your posture, the word does not return void so you do not have to worry about whether you missed it or if it will come to pass. God's word keeps and is ye and amen for your life. SHIFT!

> *Isaiah 55:11 New King James Version So shall My word be that goes forth from My mouth; It shall not return to Me void, But it shall accomplish what I please, And it shall prosper in the thing for which I sent it.*

> *2Corinthians 1:20 For all the promises of God in him are yea, and in him Amen, unto the glory of God by us.*

Journal Exploration
1. Journal two of your prophecies that have not come to pass yet or words that you are not sure if they are prophecies.
2. Journal what was occurring in your life during the time you received the word, where you received the word, and who gave you the word.
3. Journal whether they should have come to pass already or the reasons you believe they have not come to pass.
4. Spend time cleansing yourself of any anxiety and stress related to the words; cleanse of anxiety about receiving the word, them still being a work in progress, whether they are from God, and any other anxious feelings you have experienced.
5. Break soulties with the words and anyway the word itself has exalted itself above God and has become an idol where you are more focused on whether the word is of God, will come to pass, working to bring it to pass, than you are submitting to God and allowing him to bring the word to pass.
6. Spend time twice a week praise and worshipping God for ten minutes. Then spend another ten minutes in silence

submitting the words to him and waiting on him to speak. Journal what he says. If he does not say anything, do not become frustrated. Just enjoy your time with God. Remember, anytime with him is valuable. Focus on relationship and strengthening covenant and he will eventually speak regarding the words you are seeking answers for. You will also be able to receive and act on the answer he gives you. **SHIFT!**

Is It Me Discerner Nuggets

These nuggets will teach you how to properly govern God's word and discern your voice from God's voice.

When it is our voice that is speaking it is our mind, will, emotions, and soul that is talking. Often when we are dialoguing within ourselves, it is from these places which are also known as our inner man or conscience.   This dialog can be positive or negative, as such thoughts tend to stem from our experiences, issues, perceptions, influences, reactions, and responses, etc. We can even command our inner man to speak, think, and believe certain things. David commanded his soul to bless the Lord.

> *Psalms 103:1-2 Bless the Lord, O my soul: and all that is within me, bless his holy name. Bless the Lord, O my soul, and forget not all his benefits.*
>
> *Proverbs 23:7 For as he thinketh in his heart, so is he: Eat and drink, saith he to thee; but his heart is not with thee.*

Many people will say, *"I know in my heart this is God."* I would say this should be a check for you as you want to know in your spirit that it is God.

> *Proverbs 4:23 Keep thy heart with all diligence; for out of it are the issues of life.*
>
> *Jeremiah 17:9* says, The heart is deceitful above all things, and desperately sick; who can understand it?
>
> *Luke 6:24 A good man out of the good treasure of his heart bringeth forth that which is good; and an evil man out of the*

evil treasure of his heart bringeth forth that which is evil: for of the abundance of the heart his mouth speaketh.

Our heart, mind, will, and emotions can give a word that is from the well of our issues. Sometimes we fail to discern that it is not God because the word may appear reasonable, purposeful, necessary, and urgent, such that it sounds like God. Though our spirit is perfect, these areas may not be completely healed. It also requires diligence to keep them free of worldly and human influences. This is the reason they are to be subjected to our spirit man. A measure of healing can always produce a measure of truth. A measure of truth is still a lie to God. He desires us to be guided into all truth - full truth. It is important to know your issues, know where you are in your process to wholeness, and seek confirmations for words that have a measure of faith, a measure of biblical perspective, or a measure of potential to it.

> *Psalms 51:6 Behold, You desire truth in the innermost being, And in the hidden part You will make me know wisdom.*
>
> *John 16:13 Howbeit when he, the Spirit of truth, is come, he will guide you into all truth: for he shall not speak of himself; but whatsoever he shall hear, that shall he speak: and he will shew you things to come.*

We must desire full truth over our measured will. And just because a word sounds good and tickles our itchy ears, we cannot say, *"well it is not wicked or evil so it is God."*

Sometimes we become our own bewitchment when we are unable to break free from a word that is not God, and we want so desperately for it to come to pass. God is not the author of confusion, mental instability, anxiousness, or double-mindedness. *(1Corinthians 14:33, Philippians 4:6-7, James 1:8)*. There is a balance to what God speaks. Even his urgent words do not take us out of his purpose, character, nature, protection, or covering. Ezekiel and Jeremiah received some stressful words and had to release some distressing words, but the grace, character, nature, protection, and covering of God was always present. When a word is driving you where you have become obsessed with it coming to pass, and where you become irrational, impulsive, manipulative, controlling, and unstable, it is most likely a word from your own soul, will, emotions, or mind. Or it is the word of God but your obsession has caused it to become your God – your idol.

Another way to discern if it is God speaking is if there is a progression towards a successful end of what has been spoken.

> *Jeremiah 29:11 For I know the thoughts that I think toward you, saith the LORD, thoughts of peace, and not of evil, to give you an expected end.*

Sometimes we will speak a word then have to speak another one and another one in our own strength in an effort to bring it to pass. There tends to be a lot of plan B, C, D, and F's. Even if there is a concession of thoughts and instructions, what God speaks only has one plan and that is bringing it to pass through plan A. Our plans, actions, and thoughts tend to have altered instructions and tricks in an effort to produce them. They can also cycle or there is little to no progression in the word manifesting. This is different than standing in faith for a word over time. What God speaks keeps its core foundation and is constant and finite as he is.

> *Isaiah 40:8 The grass withereth, the flower fadeth: but the word of our God shall stand for ever.*

We can say one thing but do or believe another thing. God is not like this. His word is what he believes and can be confirmed by his word not returning void, by scriptures, and by his character and nature.

Journal Exploration

1. Spend time twice a week for a month dialoguing with yourself and learning the character and nature of your own voice. Examine your pitch, character, concerns, cares, desires, longings, motives, unresolved issues, resolved issues, how you view your experiences and memories, whether they are testimonies or still trigger issues for you. Journal what you learn about yourself and your voice.
2. Journal an instance where you received a word and began to implement a whole bunch of plans to bring the word to pass. Use the information in this chapter to journal what you did wrong, how you could have governed the word better, whether the word was even from God, and what occurred as a result of your actions. If the word is from God, submit the word to God for reproof and grace. Ask him for a plan in bringing the word to pass. Only do what God says. Do not add any plans to the word. Do not go ahead of God. Just do what he says and work his step by step instructions. Journal your experiences. Journal your inner thoughts, anxieties, unresolved issues, challenges, etc. Ask God to heal you of the ungodly characteristics and issues that surface. Practice this exercise as God would release future words to you. It is going to strengthen your obedience and your ability to move and SHIFT only by God's word.

VAIN HOPE
By: Taquetta Baker & Minister Reenita Keys of Kingdom Shifters Ministries

Jeremiah 23:16-18 Thus saith the Lord of hosts, Hearken not unto the words of the prophets that prophesy unto you: they make you vain: they speak a vision of their own heart, and not out of the mouth of the Lord. They say still unto them that despise me, The Lord hath said, Ye shall have peace; and they say unto every one that walketh after the imagination of his own heart, No evil shall come upon you. For who hath stood in the counsel of the Lord, and hath perceived and heard his word? who hath marked his word, and heard it?

<u>*Vain* is **habal** in the Hebrew and means:</u>
1. to be vain in act, word, or expectation; specifically to lead astray
2. to act emptily, become vain, be vain
3. to instill vain or false hope

__The Message Bible__ Don't listen to the sermons of the prophets. It's all hot air. Lies, lies, and more lies. They make it all up. Not a word they speak comes from me. They preach their 'Everything Will Turn Out Fine' sermon to congregations with no taste for God, Their 'Nothing Bad Will Ever Happen to You' sermon to people who are set in their own ways. "Have any of these prophets bothered to meet with me, the true God? bothered to take in what I have to say? listened to and then lived out my Word?

False hope - vain hope - is hope rooted in lies. The word is rooted in empty puffed up thoughts that appear to produce hope, peace, purpose and the standards of God, but have no substance or power.

- When you desire a ministry or leader to SHIFT a certain way and you release a word to appease your desires but know God did not speak this word; that is vain hope.
- When you post what you claim to be a "prophecy" on Facebook and it sounds good but God did not speak it, you just released false hope.
- When you speak a word and claim it is a "prophecy" but you just added the word prophecy to it to get likes or claps, you just released false hope.
- When you release what you contend is a "prophecy" telling someone "money cometh," they are going to have a baby, or their mate is coming, because you feel sorry for them, but God did not tell you to say that, you just released false hope.

Vain hope incites people to have faith for a matter that the word has no substance to produce.

> *Hebrews 11:1* *Now faith is the substance of things hoped for, the evidence of things not seen.*

It results in misaligning people with an empty word. They are waiting and working for manifestation that the word cannot produce.

Vain hope causes people to seek God for fruit that is not of him then when it does not manifest, it produces unbelief and sometimes anger with God. The word that you released did not come forth when you planted it. They expected God to water it and he did not because it was not of him.

The word *counsel* in *Jeremiah 23:18* is *sod* and means, *"intimacy, in close deliberation, close conversation, or secret place."* Prophecies should come from intimate interaction with the Lord.

> ➢ Your soul is self-conscious.
> ➢ Your spirit is God conscious.

If you are prophesying from your soul you are prophesying from the 2nd heaven, your own will, and intellect. This position causes you to be no different than the witches, seducers, sorcerers, diviners, and psychics.

When you are in the office of a prophet, vain hope has an even higher standard. A prophet is a man or woman who hears from God and relays to the people the mind, foresight, and future plans and purposes of the Father. Their words are from the 3rd heaven, from his spirit, and possess his mind and heart. Prophets should have a fear and reverence for God where they are cautious only to speak at his leading because they only want to speak what is of him.

God demanded the blood of Ezekiel if he did not release and handle the word properly.

> *Ezekiel 3:18 If I say to the wicked, 'You shall surely die,' and you give him no warning, nor speak to warn the wicked from his wicked way, in order to save his life, that wicked person shall die for his iniquity, but his blood I will require at your hand.*

Every word of a prophet must be carefully and properly released and must testify of Jesus. Without the fear of the Lord, a prophet can be dangerous. God may give the prophet a hard word that the people may not want to hear. But it is what they need! There is blood on the hands of prophets who release vain hope and false words rather than the pure word of the Lord.

False prophecy is not rooted in Jesus. This is why we should not test prophetic words by style, sentence structures, and vocabulary. True prophets are measured by their posture as sons. Sonship is a *noun* and prophecy is a *verb*. True prophets and prophetic people chase sonship.

> **Romans 8:15-17 The Amplified Bible** *For you have not received a spirit of slavery leading again to fear [of God's judgment], but you have received the Spirit of adoption as sons [the Spirit producing sonship] by which we [joyfully] cry, "Abba! Father!" The Spirit Himself testifies and confirms together with our spirit [assuring us] that we [believers] are children of God. And if [we are His] children, [then we are His] heirs also: heirs of God and fellow heirs with Christ [sharing His spiritual blessing and inheritance], if indeed we share in His suffering so that we may also share in His glory.*

When you are submitted in this posture, you become an authentic messenger of God rooted in his word, his purpose, his name, his glory, his inheritance, and his kingdom. Sonship reveals your identity in God. Sonship will expose who we are. Sonship SHIFTS you into a place where you are connecting to God, The Father. Often times, believers become entangled by the misplacement of their identity. When believers do not know who they are as sons, it is easy to misinterpret gifts as identity validators. The gift of prophecy does not make you a prophet. It also should not validate who you are. We should pursue sonship no matter the season and be validated through our relationship with God.

The major difference between a prophet and a diviner is sonship. Diviners are pursuing power, validation, wickedness, and an ungodly structure of sonship. They are seeking parental guidance from their gods while trying to operate in the unrepented gifts of their creator – the only true and living God. The true structure of sonship can only come from God. Those who have been rejected, ostracized, and abandoned must come into his truth so they can value and honor the worth that Jesus paid when he bled, died and rose for them to be redeemed in sonship. When we are born again, we take on the spirit of adoption. We come into our true inheritance as a son and posture in covenant relationship with our Father. It is mind-blowing how many people do not view God as a Father. Wounded believers focus on His sovereignty but never SHIFT into sonship. Since their heart is not postured in the truth of who God is, their prophetic words are contaminated with hurt religious perspectives. They may deliver an accurate word, but the delivery causes the message to become defiled. These believers may deliver a word filled with sovereignty, personal judgments, and a hardness of the heart, lacking the redemptive love of God. They may deliver words from a biased place, hurt and harsh place, but mask their insecurities by placing blame on the "anointing." In reality, God wanted to deliver the message through his heart filled with the love, empowerment, and comfort of the Father. When we do not know our identity as a son, it will cause us to deliver prophetic words that should edify, comfort, and exhort, but instead, belittle, disempower, and degrade. It also can cause us to be in total error where we release false prophecy out of an orphan spirit rather than sonship.

➤ False prophecy rebels against the authentic pure voice of God.
➤ False prophesy cannot cancel out a true prophetic word, but it can cause delays in the 2nd heaven.

➢ False prophecy is the tare that grows up to rebel against the voice of reformation.

This is the reason it is important to resist receiving vain hope and operating in vain hope. It lends way to the false. As sons, we want to establish God's truth and the fruit of his truth in the earth. Decreeing you wage war against vain hope, such that it has no room to operate in you, and you can immediately identify and nullify its workings in your life. **SHIFT!**

Journal Exploration

1. Seek God for a greater understanding of sonship and what it should look like in your life. Journal what he shares.
2. Seek God for revelation on how to posture yourself internally as a son, and practice living from your inherited position in him.
3. Repent for any ways you have released or received words of vain hope. Cleanse those words out of your life and the life of others.
4. Declare that only the true words of God are living and active in your lives and the lives of others.
5. Be careful of the words you receive. Make sure they are not words of vain hope. Ask God for a sensitivity to identify these types of words quickly, and reject them immediately so they will not delay his true words from coming forth in your life.

Discerning Masqueraders

2Corinthians 11:13-14 For such are false apostles, deceitful workers, transforming themselves into the apostles of Christ. And no marvel; for Satan himself is transformed into an angel of light. Therefore it is no great thing if his ministers also be transformed as the ministers of righteousness; whose end shall be according to their works.

<u>Righteousness is *dikaiosyne¯* in the Greek and means:</u>
1. state of him who is as he ought to be, righteousness, the condition acceptable to God
2. the doctrine concerning the way in which man may attain a state approved of God
3. integrity, virtue, purity of life, rightness, correctness of thinking feeling, and acting in a narrower sense, justice or the virtue which gives each his due

The devil can masquerade character but he cannot masquerade a Godly nature - God's identity. It may look like God, act like God, but does it have his foundation which is his word, motive, purpose, and intent, his biblical precepts - his nature.

Satan's nature is also revealed in his words.

- He is a thief, killer, and destroyer John 10:10
- He is a snake and accuser of the brethren Revelations 11:9-11
- He is a roamer and a devourer 1Peter 5:8
- He is prideful and puffed up 1Timothy 3:6, Ezekiel 28:12-14
- He is a demonic strategist, witty, deceitful, cunning, crafty, a trickster and a fraud Ephesians 6:11, 2Corinthians 2:11

- He is subtle 2Corinthians 11:3
- He is the father of lies John 3:44
- He gives fear, timidity, and anxiety 2Timothy 1:7
- He is a ruler as prince of the world Revelations 12:9-10 John 12:31
- He is the god of this age who blinds the minds of believers 2Corinthians 4:4
- He is the prince of the power of the air who works in the sons of disobedience Ephesians 2:2
- He is a murderer from the beginning and there is no truth in him John 8:44
- He is a masquerader if light and righteousness 2Corinthians 11:-13-15, Matthew 7:15, Acts 20:30
- He has power and manifests false signs and wonders that are not rooted in Godly truth or Godly nature 2Thessalonians 2:9
- He does signs that deceive even the elect Matthew 24:24
- He is a tempter Matthew 4:1-11
- He is a sifter Luke 22:31-32
- He can present as sincere and pure but is really cunning and deceitful (2Corinthians 11:3
- He leads the lawless who profess Jesus but are demonic Matthew 8:22-23
- He causes sickness and disease Luke 13:16, 2Corinthians 12:7
- He can pluck and choke out the word of God Mark 4:1-9
- He can sow tares among the word of God Matthew 13-25:30
- He imprisons people Revelations 2:10
- He has already lost the battle; he is a loser 1John 1:38, Hebrews 2:14, Colossians 2:15, Revelations 20:10

- We must resist him not agree with him James 4:7, 1Peter 5:9

The devil is your opponent. You are at war with him. Nothing he says serves you for godly gain. It is essential that you develop the skill to discern his voice and his ways. **SHIFT!**

Study Exploration
1. Study the points above regarding the nature of the devil so you can discern his voice.
2. Search God for revelation of the demons and strongholds that contend against your destiny and the prophetic words God has released in your life. Seek God for strategy on how to silence the devil and cast him out of your life.
3. Be quick to break the powers of the devil's words when they are released over you. Do not allow them to linger in your life, airways, or on frequencies. No matter who speaks them, cancel them immediately.
4. Remember you have power over the devil so do not allow him to harass you, taunt you, or speak ill of you. You have the power and the authority to tell the storms of words and terror to SHUT UP.

> *Mark 4:37-39 And there arose a great storm of wind, and the waves beat into the ship, so that it was now full. And he was in the hinder part of the ship, asleep on a pillow: and they awake him, and say unto him, Master, carest thou not that we perish? And he arose, and rebuked the wind, and said unto the sea, Peace, be still. And the wind ceased, and there was a great calm.*

Peace Be Still means to "*dumb, mute, silence, render speechless, muzzle, to be put in check.*" Know your authority and *check* the voice of the devil. **SHIFT!**

Discerning Witchcraft Words

The Holy Spirit is God's power at work. Witchcraft is the devil's, his worker's, and human beings power at work. Regular people and SAINTS (had to make that distinction clear) work witchcraft when they yield to rebellion, sin, disobedience and decisive tactics for personal gain. Sometimes people do not even know they are operating in witchcraft or being bewitched.

Saul had no clue he was engaging in witchcraft through his stubbornness and disobedience to God.

> *1Samuel 15:18-23 And the Lord sent thee on a journey, and said, Go and utterly destroy the sinners the Amalekites, and fight against them until they be consumed. Wherefore then didst thou not obey the voice of the Lord, but didst fly upon the spoil, and didst evil in the sight of the Lord? And Saul said unto Samuel, Yea, I have obeyed the voice of the Lord, and have gone the way which the Lord sent me, and have brought Agag the king of Amalek, and have utterly destroyed the Amalekites. But the people took of the spoil, sheep and oxen, the chief of the things which should have been utterly destroyed, to sacrifice unto the Lord thy God in Gilgal. And Samuel said, Hath the Lord as great delight in burnt offerings and sacrifices, as in obeying the voice of the Lord? Behold, to obey is better than sacrifice, and to hearken than the fat of rams. For rebellion is as the sin of witchcraft, and stubbornness is as iniquity and idolatry. Because thou hast rejected the word of the Lord, he hath also rejected thee from being king.*

The Galatians did not know they were being bewitched.

> *Galatians 3:1-4 O foolish Galatians, who hath bewitched you, that ye should not obey the truth, before whose eyes*

Jesus Christ hath been evidently set forth, crucified among you? This only would I learn of you, Received ye the Spirit by the works of the law, or by the hearing of faith? Are ye so foolish? having begun in the Spirit, are ye now made perfect by the flesh? Have ye suffered so many things in vain? if it be yet in vain.

You may ask, *"How does witchcraft get in the church?"* *"How do saints yield to witchcraft?"* Witchcraft can be conducted through spells, hexes, vexes, going to psychics, engaging in tarot card readings, following horoscopes, participating in yoga, etc., which we will discuss later in this book. Witchcraft can also be performed through works of the flesh, ungodly acts of disobedience, sin, stubbornness, rebellion, charismatic witchcraft, emotional manipulation, emotional and sexual seduction, acts of control, using position to control and manipulate people, using issues to play on the sympathy of people, demonic prayers, self-focused or manipulative prayers, false, erred and manipulative prophecies, inciting fear through biblical teachings that bind the freewill of others, releasing curses to keep or control members or due to being angry or frustrated with members, and lottery and gambling persuasive tactics utilized to get people to financially give. Some of these we may not even be aware that we are doing, especially if we add a scripture to it, have a valid spiritual reason for it, and believe it is in the best interest of the ministry, ourselves and our fellow brothers and sisters in Christ. We do not discern it because we do not check ourselves regarding witchcraft. So like Saul and the Galatians, we are blind to witchcraft operating in our lives and ministries.

We like to believe that we would not engage in witchcraft, but it is better to know the subtleness of it than to be so blind and self-righteousness that you succumb to it.

These are some indicators of witchcraft words.

- Manipulation – Sense of being handled, mishandled, misused, blackmailed, or swindled.
- Sense of being tossed to and fro, or swayed, or drawn unto unhealthy or ungodly practices.
- Sense of being pimped, pumped or primed.
- The word has indirect, deceptive, or abusive tactics.
- A sense of being controlled, intimidated, incanted or boxed in.
- Emotional, sexual, or physiological seduction. Sometimes you may experience uneasiness, unstable, imbalanced, discombobulated, confused, lustful, or perverted. You can be plagued with lots of emotional, irrational, stressful, anxious, traumatic, dramatic, depressed, ungodly, or sexual thoughts as it relates to the word.
- Gifts and favors being given with the word and attached to the word such that an ulterior motive has to be fulfilled. Or the gift and favor itself has a witchcraft sense that gives open access and entry to your life after taking the blessing or favor. Sometimes you can have a sense of obligation to return the gift; you feel soul tied to the person, item, or deed that was done for you. You may feel a sense of darkness around yourself or in your environment where the gift is or in your atmosphere in general. There can also be the promise of a gift or favor then it is taken away, and you are told you missed God or given conditional manipulating advances to obtain the gift or favor.
- Use of fake concern or sympathy for your wellbeing or commonality of experience to give a word to you; word can be rooted in heart and soul issues rather than from the spirit of God.

- The word can be cultivated in grandiose or seductive flattery or familiarity that is not in line with the truth of the interactions or relationship you have with that person.
- Ultimatums – uncompromising or set demands given through the word that do not have any biblical basis or is not in alignment with what God is doing or will be doing in your life.
- Victim mentalities – the word is really about the person giving it and their need to draw you into their trauma and drama and to have you doing things to fulfill their need for attention, approval, or their personal gain.
- Word is rooted in guilt trips to make you feel condemned, shamed, guilty, and obligated so you will conform.
- Confusion, twisting of words, twisting of truths – even biblical or godly truths; words that cause disorder, commotion, disturbance, agitation, frustration, instability, and altercation. Your mind, soul, heart, will, or emotions may feel like you are in a fight even though no one is physically hitting you. You have a war in your members that was placed there by the word. Sometimes darkness, gloom, and cloudiness boggles your mind and atmosphere, because of the word. You are on edge and cannot seem to get a grip on reality due to the confusion surrounding the word.
- Words that incite fear, panic, terror, dread, and death. If God releases words about death, he is revealing this so you can pray for life. Often when people only have words of this nature with no redemption attached to it, the word comes true because of the curse and demonic possession that is attached to it.
- May have a measure of doom and gloom with no hope for restoration. When God gives words of warning or urgency, it draws you to him and into his process,

progress, and success. There is also restoration attached to it.

- Feeling drained after receiving the word. It wearies you, causes you tiredness, and sucks the life out of you.
- Sense of being watched, exposed, or spiritually uncovered. This is often due to a third eye or demonic portal being attached to the word and opened up to further manipulate and control you as you agree with the word.
- The word is erred or false, but the person or devil keeps trying to get you to agree with the word.
- Telepathy – Sensing as if you are getting signals, impressions or pressure from an unseen force after being given a word. Sense of information being transferred into your mind to get you to adhere to the word. Feelings of a spear being lodged into your head and brain to block normal processing, or a vice grip device being locked onto your brain or side of your head that is attempting to control your thoughts or actions, or interject thoughts and behaviors.
- Necromancy – Using spirits of the dead to convey information, particularly about your future or something that is important to you.
- Words obtained through sorcery, divination, magic, Wicca, spell casting, hexes, vexes, potions, rituals, good luck charms, demonology, or Satanism, is witchcraft; Seeking or receiving words from mediums, spiritualist, idolatrous priests, white witches, black witches, good witches, or warlocks, is witchcraft; words released through psychic readings and tarot cards is witchcraft (*Leviticus 19:31, Leviticus 20:27, Deuteronomy 18:10-12*).
- Receiving words through vibes, energies, the universe, mother earth, the stars, and the moon through worshiping of the host of heaven (*2Kings 17:16*).

Yoga, Christian Yoga – Yoga is rooted in Hinduism and Spiritualism. Yoga practitioners encourage you to empty your mind; to release to a place of a blank mind. God tells us to have his mind and to meditate on him day and night. Even if you contend you are meditating on God, your positions say you are bowing to a Hindu God. Every pose has symbolism that is tied to mysticism, idol gods and demonic spirits. The quest of yoga is to be able to reach a height of meditation where you can perform unexplainable supernatural poses that demonstrate how energy forces of peace, light, enlightenment, and power have overtaken your body, spirit, and life. What really has happened is spirits have entered your body through your mediation and surrender into spiritual realms and has given you formation power to do such unique poses. It is no way to make yoga godly because its source is from demonic realms. If you are utilizing the practices of yoga to obtain a word from God, you are engaging in witchcraft. The source of the word is not Jesus Christ but is whatever God you have exposed yourself to as you meditate and engage in the poses techniques. Meditation in and of itself is not wrong or idolatrous. However, meditation that is not centered on God or his word can be dangerous, especially when you are so relaxed you enter spiritual realms or spheres of unconsciousness or subconsciousness within your brain. There are 33 million idol gods in Hinduism. They have an idol god for everything that you need or desire. When you are engaging in yoga, you are offering up a sacrifice upon an idolatrous altar as that is the main purpose of the practice, the meditations, and the positions. Therefore, you are drawing enlightenment, peace, strength, relief, and healing, from whatever it is you are needing and desiring in your life at that time, as all sacrifices produce a transference from the person to the god and vice versa. One thing we must understand about God is just because we think we are engaging him; does not mean he is engaging us. God does not accept strange fire no matter how we package it. He may not strike us dead like he did people in the Old Testament times, but he still will not receive an offering from the altar of idolatry.

One main stronghold spirit of yoga is the Kundalini demon which is often discerned in ministry events, especially during high times of worship and crowded altar calls. The Kundalini demon in yoga is a female energy serpent type spirit that lies coiled at the base of the spine. It comes in through yoga practices and even practices of mediation that open demonic realms rather than realms of God. Often people are so addicted to the feeling of worship itself that it has become God in their life. They are not having encounters with God, but with how the atmosphere and presence of the glory make them feel. When worship itself becomes their God, it SHIFTS a person into vain imaginations where they begin to have encounters in realms that they think are heaven or heavenly, or of God, but are really spiritual realms that are free access to anyone. Because they are in a vulnerable state of worship and are not discerning, they encounter demonic spirits who pose as angels of light and thus open the door to kundalini and all types of other spirits. Spirits of Pharmacia operate in these realms which is the reason many people will appear intoxicated or high during and after worship but reveal no true transformation, and no real encounter of revelations with the spirit of God. **Though not always the case,** they only tend to speak about how great the encounter was, with no reverence or fear of the Lord, no download of word, strategy, knowledge, or revelation, deliverance, healing, or no tangible change in their lives. Even days after such a major encounter, they do not seem to have any revelation from God for what the purpose was and what changed in them. I am not saying you should always have revelation, but when you are having such encounters all the time with no word or transformation to SHIFT your life, you are just smoking glory – similar to a person smoking crack, marijuana or using prescription drugs to get high. Such experiences are yoga-like practices that open your spirit and life to witchcraft practices and demonization. Sadly, many are not even aware that they are bound because these acts occurred during ministry events.

- Moses received his purpose of delivering the Israelites after the burning bush, his face would be white as snow that it brought fear and reverence to the Israelites when he left the glory of God, and he wrote the Ten Commandments when encountering God (*Exodus 34:29-35*).
- Isaiah was saying "woe is me" after his awe striking encounter in the glory; he was full of repentance and fear of the Lord (*Isaiah 6*).
- Ezekiel received prophecies while being in the spirit realm with the Lord (**Ezekiel 3:24, 37:1-14**).
- Paul did not know if he was in the body or out of it, but he received such powerful revelation that God buffeted him to keep him humbled (*2Corinthians 12:3*).

It is important to make sure your divine visitations and encounters are being God led, God-focused, and producing of God revelation, enlightenment, strategy, transformation, etc. Make sure you have the fruit and spirit of God that attest to the visitations that you contend are of God.

Witchcraft will be released at an enormous rate in the coming days. There will be divination and dimensions of witchcraft released that has not been revealed yet. There is an increase of people becoming witches and warlocks and this is becoming a norm. There is and will continue to be an increase of people declaring they are Christian witches and warlocks; this will be received as the lines of biblical standards become blurred, devalued, and outlawed. Vain hope will sway you if you cannot discern the voice of witchcraft. It is time out for being scared of witchcraft, witches, warlocks, and scared to confront and overthrow it.

> *Ephesians 4:14* *That we henceforth be no more children, tossed to and fro, and carried about with every wind of doctrine, by the sleight of men, and cunning craftiness, whereby they lie in wait to deceive.*

> *The Amplified Bible* *So that we are no longer children [spiritually immature], tossed back and forth [like ships on a stormy sea] and carried about by every wind of [shifting] doctrine, by the cunning and trickery of [unscrupulous] men, by the deceitful scheming of people ready to do anything [for personal profit].*

It is time to mature and overthrow the true enemies of God. Especially those that would release doctrines upon the wind that would SHIFT people from the truth of God.

Study Exploration
1. Do not just read but STUDY this chapter in detail, especially the discerners regarding the voice of witchcraft.
2. Conduct a bible study and an online study on witchcraft, witches, warlocks, and idolatry.

Freewill To Hear And Obey

Though there are times the Lord will give commands, rebukes, chastisement, make blanket statements, or blatant references when obedience is essential to our protection, progress, and well-being, as this is a father's role in a child's life. We are children of our God. However, often God speaks in a manner that gives us choice and free will. His heart and nature are for us to choose him because we want relationship, not because he demanded us. That is why *John 4:24* says, *"those that worship."* Worship is a posture of freewill; total surrendering of our will and life to God. It is not just an act or series of tasks and behaviors, but a lifestyle choice that is revealed as we walk in relationship with him. Therefore:

- We may hear words or statements in our spirit like, *"I think the Lord wants me to do this or that."*
- God may have dialog where he is posing his will or way to us for consideration and further pondering.
- God may reveal his standards and then give us a choice to choose.
- God may share his truth on the matter which often can be confirmed through the Bible.
- God will share his thoughts then give you a strong impression in your spirit on what to do or what his will and purpose is.
- God will give you a conviction on the matter then you know it is him.
- God will put his desires in you; *Psalm 37:4* says, *"Delight thyself also in the LORD; and he shall give thee the desires of thine heart."*
- God may simply speak his answer, truth, or purpose directly into our spirit which strengthens us and causes us to become keener as we mature in relationship with him.

Study Exploration

1. Journal warnings, rebukes, and words of correction that God has given you over the years and how you have responded.
2. Highlight areas where you did not listen, was slow to adhere, or dreaded having to be obedient to the word. Spend time exploring and journaling the underlying issues of the reasons you responded in the manner in which you did.
3. Ask God to deliver and heal these areas in you.

The Blockage Of A Strong Will

God loves when we ask his point of view on a matter. It shows that we want to please him. It demonstrates that we want to represent him and be conduits of him in the earth. More importantly, it reveals that we want to be guided into all truth.

> *John 16:13 Howbeit when he, the Spirit of truth, is come, he will guide you into all truth: for he shall not speak of himself; but whatsoever he shall hear, that shall he speak: and he will shew you things to come.*

Sometimes our will (our conscious power and right to choose), or our flesh is so strong that we think we are hearing from God but it is really us leading us - us being our own god.

When we are strong-willed, we are determined to do what we want and get what we want regardless to what God or others advise.

Dictionary.com synonyms for *strong willed*: determined, resolute, stubborn, obstinate, willful, headstrong, strong-minded, self-willed, unbending, unyielding, set in purpose or opinion.

Taquetta's synonyms:
- Rebellious; anti-submissive or submissive when it is convenient or is in line with one's needs or desires.
- Risk taking with little to no regard of consequences.
- Will sacrifice others and the greater good for the sake of being right.
- Thrill seekers, adrenaline rushers.

- Loves how it feels to have desires fulfilled such that it is more of a lust than a balanced part of life; it becomes a driven zealous importance.
- Thrives to be the center of attention and be spotlighted.
- Prideful self-boasters rooted in insecurity or a need to prove one's worth, value, ability, or capability.
- Destined to succeed but the drive for success overrides the process of success.

Our will can be so strong that we literally think it is God speaking, but it is our own desires governing our lives. It makes it difficult for us to hear truth from God and for others, and often we use the Bible, signs of the world, and happenstances to further confirm our will. Because God does not override our will, we lack conviction and assume God is in agreement with our will. But really a strong will is like a fortified wall. It blocks out the truth and voice of the Lord. What made David special to God is that he always sought to break his will to be full of God.

>   **Psalms 51:17** *The sacrifices of God are a broken spirit: a broken and a contrite heart, O God, thou wilt not despise.*

David delighted in the will of God.

>   **Psalms 40:8** *I delight to do thy will, O my God: yea, thy law is within my heart.*

Jesus feasted on God and declared, "My meat is to do the will of him that sent me, and to finish his work (**John 4:34**).

Jesus' lifestyle was to please and live the will of God.

John 5:30 I can of mine own self do nothing: as I hear, I judge: and my judgment is just; because I seek not mine own will, but the will of the Father which hath sent me.

Jesus knew that his purpose was to do the will of God.

John 6:38 For I came down from heaven, not to do mine own will, but the will of him that sent me.

Even as you seek God for his heart, mind, thoughts, and desires, seek him for his will and purpose for your life. Seek God for a love of his will and purpose and delight in who he is saying you are to be and live his will out loud in daily obedience, surrendering and submission. This helps to not only hear the voice of God but to SHIFT you into becoming the voice of God made flesh to all man.

This also postures you only to do things when you clearly know he is speaking. The stubbornness of your will becomes to hear God and only do what he says. And you will not budge until you receive a clearing from him.

Study Exploration
1. Examine your life and journal areas that are not totally surrendered to God.
2. Journal and address any disobedience, lawlessness, anti-submissiveness, stubbornness, rebellion, control, self-will, pride, and manipulation, that hinders you from being immediately obedient to God. Break these strongholds personally and generationally, and cast out any spirit operating in your soul, heart, mind, emotions, and will regarding them.
3. Spend time daily surrendering your will to God and asking him to renew your heart and spirit, and make your will contrite before him.

4. Ask for a heart to love the things he loves and to hate the things he hates so that your will is to do what pleases him.

Testing The Word

It is important to test the spirit of a word.

> *1John 4:1-5 Beloved, believe not every spirit, but try the spirits whether they are of God: because many false prophets are gone out into the world. Hereby know ye the Spirit of God: Every spirit that confesseth that Jesus Christ is come in the flesh is of God: And every spirit that confesseth not that Jesus Christ is come in the flesh is not of God: and this is that spirit of antichrist, whereof ye have heard that it should come; and even now already is it in the world. Ye are of God, little children, and have overcome them: because greater is he that is in you, than he that is in the world. They are of the world: therefore speak they of the world, and the world heareth them.*

As I considered this scripture, the Holy Spirit revealed to me that when I receive a word and am not sure it is of God, I can ask *"did Jesus come in the flesh?"* Demons will not confess this but the Holy Spirit and my own voice will. You can then test whether it is your own voice versus God's voice by identifying the motives, intent, and heart of the matter at hand.

The most essential motive is whether it glorifies God. It is important to make sure the word glorifies God in every way. Not in some ways, not measured glory, not compromised glory that does not eventually produce full glory, but in every way that edifies and exalts him. There should not be any measure of defamation, reproach, blasphemy, sin, or transgression if it is God speaking.

> *1Thessalonians 5:19-23 Quench not the Spirit. Despise not prophesyings. Prove all things; hold fast that which is good.*

Abstain from all appearance of evil. And the very God of peace sanctify you wholly; and I pray God your whole spirit and soul and body be preserved blameless unto the coming of our Lord Jesus Christ.

It is also important that the word embodies the character **AND** nature of God as many things appear to have the character of God; it may appear integral, morally correct or appropriate, righteous, just, reasonable, logical, but does it have his nature. His nature are his laws, standards, and identity. I am only going to put a few scriptures as you can do a google search on the nature of God and study scriptures on the topic.

> **James 3:17 The Amplified Bible** *But the wisdom from above is first of all pure (undefiled); then it is peace-loving, courteous (considerate, gentle). [It is willing to] yield to reason, full of compassion and good fruits; it is wholehearted and straightforward, impartial and unfeigned (free from doubts, wavering, and insincerity).*

> **Philippians 4:8** *Finally, brethren, whatsoever things are true, whatsoever things are honest, whatsoever things are just, whatsoever things are pure, whatsoever things are lovely, whatsoever things are of good report; if there be any virtue, and if there be any praise, think on these things.*

> **1Peter 1:15-17** *But as he which hath called you is holy, so be ye holy in all manner of conversation; Because it is written, Be ye holy; for I am holy.*

> **1Corinthians 14:3** *But he that prophesieth speaketh unto men to edification, and exhortation, and comfort.*

Jeremy 29:11 For I know the thoughts that I think toward you, says the Lord, thoughts of peace and not of evil, to give you a future and a hope.

God's nature is to chastise those he loves so be open to words of correction. Do not ignore words that come to warn, provoke repentance, expose a character flaw, incite deliverance or healing. God's nature is always to restore you into his original likeness before the fall of Adam and Eve.

Proverbs 3:11-12 My son, despise not the chastening of the Lord; neither be weary of his correction: For whom the Lord loveth he correcteth; even as a father the son in whom he delighteth.

Hebrews 12:4-6 Ye have not yet resisted unto blood, striving against sin. And ye have forgotten the exhortation which speaketh unto you as unto children, My son, despise not thou the chastening of the Lord, nor faint when thou art rebuked of him: For whom the Lord loveth he chasteneth, and scourgeth every son whom he receiveth.

The Tester! *(To be used when you need to try the spirit of a word).*
1. *Examine* – Inspect carefully; inquire and investigate the voice that is speaking.
    o Is it God, man, witches, warlocks, or devils speaking?
    o Examine the source, the root, and motives.
    o Examine the knowledge, reactions, and qualifications of the word.
    o Who gave the word? What is their character and life like? Do they have the character and nature of God? If not, do they have an ulterior motive for sharing the word? God can use strangers and ungodly people. Usually they are unaware

he is using them and have no motive behind what they are speaking.

o What was the purpose the word was given?
o Does the word seduce, flatter, control, manipulate, or puff up?
o Does it steal, kill, or destroy anything that God desires to live and multiply?
o Does the word violate your will, violate biblical standards, violate God?
o Is it more than a good word; is it godly?
o Does it guide you into all truth or does it guide you away from God and his will?
o Does it confess of the Lordship of Jesus Christ? If so, was there any resistance, shuttering, cringing and anguish as you tried the word and/or person with Jesus name?

2. *Scrutinize* – Search the word out before God.
   o Surveillance its character, nature, genuineness, and substance.
   o Consider what atmosphere the word was given in (was it a God encounter, Facebook post or live, ministry event, in the community, middle of a conversation, dream, vision, prayer, study of the word).
   o Did you share personal information before the word was given? Scrutinize with God if this had any bearing on what was released to you.
     ▪ Sympathy – person had feelings or impulses of compassion, sorrow, pity for you so they released a word to you.
     ▪ Empathy - person identifying with your experience and then giving you a word in hopes of encouraging you.

- Really God – person focused attentively and did not allow their sympathy or empathy for you to sway their spirit. Spoke only what God said. You are able to identify their encouragement, sympathy, and empathy from the word of God. Or it was so mixed into the encounter, you are not sure.

3. *Prove* – Establish the truth, evidence, and argument of the word.
    - Does it align to scripture?
    - Does it align with what God already said?
    - Is it a new progressive word to add to what God has said?
    - Is it the proper season for the word or for future seasons?
    - Does it align with the expected end that God has spoken?
    - Does it glorify God and advance his kingdom?
    - Are there any lies, contradictions, errors, mixed truths to the word?
    - Does it bring confusion and mixture to what God has already said?

4. *Try* – Test the effect or result of the word by spiritually examining it for godly fruit.
    - When you consider it before God, is it empty or can it create?
    - Is what it created of God, the devil, or man?
    - Does it produce godly fruit, bad fruit, unhealthy fruit, contaminated fruit, diseased fruit, murderous fruit?
    - Who benefits when it produces?

- Will it transform lives, lands, regions, or spheres?
- Does what it produce draw people to God, man, or you?
- Is it worthy to bear God's name and kingdom?

Demonic Infiltrators Of God's Word
By: Taquetta Baker & Minister Reenita Keys of Kingdom Shifters Ministries

Diviners, Sorcerers, High Priest, Witches, Warlocks - Can hear from the 3rd heaven, but they operate from the 2nd heaven. Many of them are falling prophets who still possess the gift and mantle but do not have their heavenly authority. They, therefore, can access words that have already been released from the third heaven and are on the frequencies and airwaves of the 1st, 2nd, and 3rd heaven.

> *Romans 11:29 For the gifts and calling of God are without repentance.*

Unbelief and Doubt – Speak distrust and doubt to cause a person to question, be suspicious of, fear, or reject the true word of God. Many of the interjections are due to a lack of faith and sometimes sound reasonable, but lack faith and trust in God. Inability to walk by faith or journey in faith until substance manifests. Will want you to reject God until manifestation prevails.

> *Hebrews 11:1 Now faith is the substance of things hoped for, the evidence of things not seen.*

Naysayers – Habitually express negative or pessimistic views about God, his body, and his word. Constantly speak unhopeful, joyless, doom type words to cast doubt and gloom on the true word of God. Do not want people to believe in prophecy or anything about God that does not have what they consider physically tangible evidence (*Study Exodus 3-4*). Naysayers will also try to publicly embarrass you for believing a word of God. They will get you before people and then speak of your prophecy and ridicule, drill, and question what God has spoken. Their purpose is to get you to reject what God is speaking and to scorn you for holding fast to the prophetic word.

> **Matthew 10:18-20 (English Standard Bible)** *And you will be dragged before governors and kings for my sake, to bear witness before them and the Gentiles. When they deliver you over, do not be anxious how you are to speak or what you are to say, for what you are to say will be given to you in that hour. For it is not you who speak, but the Spirit of your Father speaking through you.*

Debaters – Cause to debate, test, and prove the word based on doctrine and ideologies that oppose the true word and prophetic authority and power of God (Study Noah). The quarreling is more for entertainment purposes as they mock your belief and stance than truly wanting to learn, change and understand what God has spoken or will do in your life. Strive to get you out of character so they can prove that you are not godly and neither are your beliefs.

> **Titus 3:9** - *But avoid foolish questions, and genealogies, and contentions, and strivings about the law; for they are unprofitable and vain.*

Mockers & Scorners – Laughs and pock fun for standing on God's prophecies. Will cause psychological warfare of fear in making you believe you will fail or that God is not going to show up and fulfill his promises for you. Jeremiah had mockers. They were mocking and beckoning God to follow through with releasing wrath upon them. People mock Jesus' return. Sigh!!!!!

> **Jeremiah 17:15** *Listen to what they are saying to me. They are saying, "Where are the things the LORD threatens us with? Come on! Let's see them happen!"*

Psalms 1:1 Blessed is the man that walketh not in the counsel of the ungodly, nor standeth in the way of sinners, nor sitteth in the seat of the scornful.

2Peter 3:3-4 Knowing this first, that there shall come in the last days scoffers, walking after their own lusts, And saying, Where is the promise of his coming? for since the fathers fell asleep, all things continue as they were from the beginning of the creation.

Deuteronomy 31:6 Be strong and of a good courage, fear not, nor be afraid of them: for the LORD thy God, he it is that doth go with thee; he will not fail thee, nor forsake thee.

Psychological Warfare (Study the story of Nehemiah) – Derives from territorial spirits, powers, spells and word curses, and witchcraft sent from witches, warlocks, and demonic chatter from demons, ungodly, foolish, or ignorant, people. Words live on airways and demons pick them up, especially the negative ones then speak them back to you to distract, weary and kill your progress or stance in God. This warfare causes anxiety, insecurity, and a wrestling and questioning of God's word. Break the powers of wrestling and questioning. Blatantly muzzle and silence demonic voices by telling them to SHUT UP! Break the powers of spells, sooth saying, psychic powers and telepathy being sent against you. Use the blood of Jesus to cleanse airways and frequencies of ungodly, negative, and demonic words that have been spoken about you.

Ezekiel 8:12 Then He said to me, "Son of man, do you see what the elders of the house of Israel are committing in the dark, each man in the room of his carved images? For they say, 'The LORD does not see us; the LORD has forsaken the land.*

Ephesians 6:12 For our struggle is not against flesh and blood, but against the rulers, against the powers, against the world forces of this darkness, against the spiritual forces of wickedness in the heavenly places.

False Prophecy – Prophetic words that contradict the true word of God. They cause confusion, double-mindedness, spiritual schizophrenia, and false hope. Makes it difficult for people to discern God's word from lies. They lead people from the truth and cause them to believe and trust in lies.

Matthew 7:15-16 Beware of the false prophets, who come to you in sheep's clothing, but inwardly are ravenous wolves. "You will know them by their fruits. Grapes are not gathered from thorn bushes nor figs from thistles, are they?

Jeremiah 28:15 Then Jeremiah the prophet said to Hananiah the prophet, "Listen now, Hananiah, the LORD has not sent you, and you have made this people trust in a lie.

Spirit Of Error - Twist prophetic scriptures and cause misinterpretation and misinterpretation of what God is saying. Picking and choosing what is deemed "valid' and misrepresenting or mishandling the message God was speaking.

Mark 12:24 Jesus said to them, "Is this not the reason you are mistaken, that you do not understand the Scriptures or the power of God?

1John 4:6 We are from God; he who knows God listens to us; he who is not from God does not listen to us By this we know the spirit of truth and the spirit of error.

Idolatry - Comes to entice and trick people into listening to, serving, worshipping, and offering up sacrifices unto another god so they will abort the word of the true and living God.

Spirit of Oppression & Depression – While people are holding fast to the prophetic word, this spirit causes them to be depressed and melancholy, and will cause them to experience withdrawal, tiredness, weightiness, pressure, hopelessness, helplessness, and suicidal thoughts, making it difficult with having to trust, work, or wait on the word to come to pass.

> *Mark 4:18-19 Still others, like seed sown among thorns, hear the word; 19 but the worries of this life, the deceitfulness of wealth and the desires for other things come in and choke the word, making it unfruitful.*

Spirits of the Past – Stifles the prophetic word by bringing up the past, especially past failures or challenging experiences. Often comes through familiar family spirits, close relatives and friends who do not have a strong relationship with the Lord, lack of faith or a true understanding of living by the word of God, and jealous people who want others to fail.

> *Philippians 3:13-14 Brothers, I do not consider that I have made it my own. But one thing I do: forgetting what lies behind and straining forward to what lies ahead, I press on toward the goal for the prize of the upward call of God in Christ Jesus.*

> *Isaiah 43:18-19 Remember not the former things, nor consider the things of old. Behold, I am doing a new thing; now it springs forth, do you not perceive it? I will make a way in the wilderness and rivers in the desert.*

2Corinthians 5:17 Therefore, if anyone is in Christ, he is a new creation. The old has passed away; behold, the new has come.

Orphan Spirit - Wars against prophetic words. Paints ungodly imaginations and instills lies filled with inadequacy and unworthiness regarding what God is speaking. Causes an abortion of true sonship. When not aligned with true sonship it is easy to believe words will not come to pass, the word was for someone else, or feel undeserving of the word. Causes warfare against identity where a person cannot connect and embrace the prophetic words. Orphan spirit often tag teams with the spirit of rejection and the vagabond spirit.

Romans 8:15 The Amplified Bible For [the Spirit which] you have now received [is] not a spirit of slavery to put you once more in bondage to fear, but you have received the Spirit of adoption [the Spirit producing sonship] in [the bliss of] which we cry, Abba (Father)! Father!

Spirit of Pride – Puffed up, vain, ego tripping, self-exalted, conceited, haughty, stubborn, rebellious, haughty in heart, aggressive, easily enraged, self-righteous in one's character. Not willing to be corrected when in error concerning a word. Does not care about the character or nature to which a word is released, how it impacts people and ministries or how it represents God.

Proverbs 16:18 Pride goeth before destruction, and an haughty spirit before a fall.

Spirit of Rebellion – Provokes people to be anti-submissive to the word of God and receiving the word of God. Provokes prophets and prophetic people to be anti-submissive and nonconforming to leadership and to God. Tend to be flighty, renegade, aggressive, defensive, and resistant in releasing the word of God without any regard to order, protocol, or submitting their gift to accountability. Postures the prophetic inside the 1st and 2nd heaven where it becomes witchcraft and divination due to being rooted in self-focused, self-willed, selfish, and prideful motives.

> *1Samuel 15:23 For rebellion is as the sin of witchcraft, and stubbornness is as iniquity and idolatry. Because thou hast rejected the word of the Lord, he hath also rejected thee from being king.*

> *Proverbs 17:11 Evil people are eager for rebellion, but they will be severely punished.*

Spirit of Vagabond – Wander from place to place receiving words, but never settling in God to see them come to pass. Drain prophets and prophetic people by constantly receiving the same word with minimal to no activation of what is being spoken. Lives life postured in rejection, self-rejection, and fear of rejection, ostracism, and false hope – empty and because of unresolved issues, there is an inability to maintain and sustain the substance of God's truth and creative words.

> *Genesis 4:14 Behold, thou hast driven me out this day from the face of the earth; and from thy face shall I be hid; and I shall be a fugitive and a vagabond in the earth; and it shall come to pass, that every one that findeth me shall slay me.*

> *Psalms 109:10 Let his children be continually vagabonds, and beg: let them seek their bread also out of their desolate places.*

Spirit of Rejection – Causes people to reject the word of God, the prophetic gift, prophetic office, and those being used to release God's word. Causes prophets and prophetic people to fear being rejected so they coward with releasing words.

> *Matthew 10:14 And whosoever shall not receive you, nor hear your words, when ye depart out of that house or city, shake off the dust of your feet.*

Spirit Of Mammon - Fights the prosperity, fruit, multiplication, and legacy of prophetic words. Uses words of God for financial gain. Attaches prophecies and words of God to money, material gain, and success so people will think ill of them, view them as divination and worldliness, and not want to receive them. Manipulate and seduce people out of their money by charging them for words of God. Make them feel they will not succeed, progress, or be cared for if they do not give. Have people focused on the lust of the eyes, lust of the flesh, and the prides of life rather than the kingdom and covenant of God. Attempts to get people to serve the god of money rather than the true and living God.

> *Matthew 6:24 No one can serve two masters; for either he will hate the one and love the other, or else he will be loyal to the one and despise the other. You cannot serve God and mammon.*

> *Matthew 6:19-21 Do not lay up for yourselves treasures on earth, where moth and rust destroy and where thieves break in and steal; but lay up for yourselves treasures in heaven, where neither moth nor rust destroys and where thieves do not break in and steal. For where your treasure is, there your heart will be also.*

Spirit of Dissatisfaction & Gluttony - Become familiar with the voice of God. Cause the receiver to believe their word was not that big of a deal and there is a much "bigger word" they can get from God. Provokes comparison, envy, lust, overindulgence, and compulsiveness, where the person is dull to the fruit and substance of the word. Rather than activate it, constant thirst and feasting for words manifest. This is one of the reasons why certain people keep going back and forth into prophetic lines getting all the words they can. This spirit creates unsatisfaction, where the person is always receiving and seeking, yet never being fulfilled or postured to receive fulfillment of what God is speaking for their lives.

> *Deuteronomy 21:20 They shall say to the elders, "This son of ours is stubborn and rebellious. He will not obey us. He is a glutton and a drunkard."*

> *Philippians 3:19 Their destiny is destruction, their god is their stomach, and their glory is in their shame. Their mind is set on earthly things.*

Spirit of Python - Restricts and squeezes out the word of God. Restricts the prophetic word from going forth in ministries and prophetic people. Attacks prophets with the attempt to suffocate the prophetic voice of God. Sales the prophetic word for gain. Attempts to fit in with those who have the true word of God so it can snuff out God's prophetic word with ungodly words. Tied to the spirit of death and necromancy. Uses spirits of the dead to speak familiar words while making people believe these words are from the Lord.

> *Acts 16:16-18 Once when we were going to the place of prayer, we were met by a female slave who had a spirit by which she predicted the future. She earned a great deal of money for her owners by fortune-telling. She followed Paul and the rest of us, shouting, "These men are servants of the Most High God, who are telling you the way to be saved." She kept this up for many days. Finally Paul became so annoyed that he turned around and said to the spirit, "In the*

name of Jesus Christ I command you to come out of her!" At
that moment the spirit left her.

Spirit of Leviathan - Twists and causes confusion in
communicating God's word accurately.

> *Job 41:1 Can you draw out Leviathan with a fishhook? Or
> press down his tongue with a cord? "Can you put a rope in
> his nose Or pierce his jaw with a hook? "Will he make many
> supplications to you, Or will he speak to you soft words?*

Spirit of Jezebel (Study Story of Elijah) - Seduces,
manipulates, and controls with lustful, enticing, flattering, and
false words.

> *Revelation 2:20 Notwithstanding I have a few things
> against thee, because thou sufferest that woman Jezebel,
> which calleth herself a prophetess, to teach and to seduce my
> servants to commit fornication, and to eat things sacrificed
> unto idols.*

Study Exploration
1. Examine and journal experiences you have had with these
    infiltrators. Highlight times, seasons, and ways in which
    they tend to infiltrate your life so that you can be conscious
    of this in future seasons.
2. Familiarize yourself with these infiltrators so you can
    identify them when you encounter them.

Wisdom Keys For Releasing Prophetic Words Properly

- When God gives you a word do not add to it or take away from it, even when people try to pry you for more information. You especially want to adhere to this if you know that word itself causes character challenges for you, makes you want to let someone have it, is a pet peeve for you, or triggers sensitive or unhealed areas for you. Tell the person to take the word to God for further understanding. This keeps you from speaking something you should not have spoken, or from behaving in a way that would cause a person to question whether the word came from God.

- Seek confirmation and wise counsel for words that are rebukes, cautions, or warnings, especially for people who are leaders or are not under your spiritual covering or jurisdiction. You need wisdom of how or whether to release the word and how to present it where it will be considered or received.

- Sometimes God may want to pray rather than share a word, or he may be simply revealing his heart to you. Be slow to share just because you hear. Make sure it is the correct timing, season, and his leading. Make sure you let people know if the word is for now or later. If you do not know, encourage them to seek God for proper timing to release the word.

- Sometimes it can be God speaking but your lack of maturity, wisdom, compassion, or unresolved issues, can cause you to mishandle the word or display character issues that diminish the power and miraculous vigor of the word. Moses was an example of this. He became angry at the Israelites, and struck the rock when he should have spoke to it so that water could be provided for the people. His poor character caused him to not enter the promise land. Do not be so focused on maturing your gift that you do not mature in your character and receive healing of wounds. Maturity and healing are vital keys to effectively handling the word of the Lord.

- Do not allow the praise and accolades of the people to steward the word that you are releasing. It is easy to SHIFT into a word of flesh and even want validation of people when you are allowing the emotions of the people to dictate the prophetic release. Make sure you have a healthy identity so you will only desire validation from God.

- Be confident in your relationship with the Lord where you are not allowing fear to muzzle your mouth. The enemy will fight your prophetic release by sending psychological warfare to silence your voice. Trust that if you open your mouth, he will fill it.

- Please know that public prophecies SHIFT and guide peoples' lives, atmospheres, movements and visions of their ministry. When these words are not judged, people are made to believe they are true, or made to agree with them when they are not of God. It can quench the Holy Spirit and the direction of God for that service, the ministry, and the vision. I have been in a ministry service where we constantly cycled due to the swaying of words by prophets that had their own motive, but because of who they were and their position, what they said was never tested. Check your motives before releasing public words. Be honest with yourself and test your own spirit. If you are not completely sure that it is not your desires or soul at work, hold the word until you can test it in your prayer time with the Lord.

BOOK REFERENCES

- *Blueletterbible.com*

- *Biblestudytools.com*

- *Dictionary.com*

- *Olivetree.com*

- *Strong's Exhaustive Bible Concordance Online Bible Study Tools*

- *Wikipedia*

  - ❖ *Front Book cover photo by Tashema Davis. Connect with her via Facebook.*

  - ❖ *Cover photo by Reenita Keys. Connect with her via Facebook.*

  - ❖ *Editing by Nina Cook & Amanda Latrice. Connect with them via Facebook.*

Kingdom Shifters Books & Apparel
Available at Kingdomshifters.com

BOOKS FOR EVERYONE

Healing The Wounded Leader
Kingdom Shifters Decree That Thang
There Is An App For That
Kingdom Watchman Builder On The Wall
Embodiment Of A Kingdom Watchman
Dismantling Homosexuality Handbook
Release The Vision
Kingdom Heirs Decree That Thang
Birthing Books That Shift Generations

Let There Be Sight
Atmosphere Changers (Weaponry)
Apostolic Governing
Apostolic Mantle
Dance From Heaven To Earth
Annihilating Church Hurt
Discerning The Voice of God
Prayers That Shift Atmospheres
Feasting In His Presence

BOOKS FOR DANCERS
Dancers! Dancers! Dancers! Decree That Thang
Spirits That Attack Dance Ministers & Ministries
Dance & Fivefold Ministry
Dance From Heaven To Earth

CD'S
Decree That Thang CD
Kingdom Heirs Decree That Thang CD
Teaching & Worship CD's

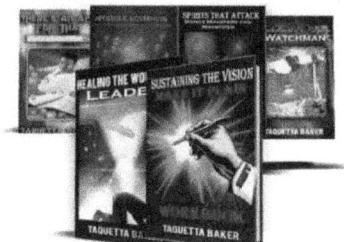

www.ingramcontent.com/pod-product-compliance
Lightning Source LLC
LaVergne TN
LVHW091313080426
835510LV00007B/478